Boardroom Culture Shock

7 STRATEGIES TO AMPLIFY THE COMPETENCE AND CAPACITY OF BOARD CULTURE

Charline E. Manuel

Author of *The Power of One Accord*

Dedicated to those who invest their time, talent, and resources serving on boards of mission driven organizations.

CONTENT

INTRODUCTION

Shock is a strong word. It can cause alarm, distress, or a jolt that tampers with the status quo. The word can also carry a positive connotation such as surprise, amazement, and tampering with the status quo in a good way. The culture shock we speak of in this book is to draw attention to some of the traditional ways under which boards have functioned in the past that may be ripe for change. Our purpose is to inspire a fresh look at methods of board service that build on the past, raise board performance, and increase capacity, all while being responsive to changing communities and a shifting global environment.

The goal of this book is to help boards review the culture that dictates how they function. Some of the topics covered are those that are often avoided, glossed-over or by-passed as not urgent enough to spend time on. However, by addressing these topics, a conscious decision can be made for reshaping, upgrading, or altogether transforming, that which drives the quality of decisions made in the boardroom.

For some boards, just having the discussion of shifting the culture will cause alarm and distress. Culture can be a sacred thing. It is how we do what we've always done. It reveals our guiding values, strategies, and beliefs we hold dear. It's our comfort food, our cool drink on a hot summer day, or it's the contentment we find listening to a favorite piece of music we never grow tired of. Having an established culture gives us history, tradition, and shapes the implementation of the rules we live by. Now I know, culture shock may not be what most board members sign up for. I hope there is comfort in knowing that in this book we're talking reshaping culture, not destroying it.

Over the past twenty years, the number of nonprofit organizations has increased in number by over fifty percent. This means that more people than ever before are seated at boardroom tables guiding organizations that have the charge and opportunity to make a difference in the affairs of peoples' lives. Historically, boards were mostly composed of a group of members that were familiar with each other, predominately white males, financially well-off, and who wanted to do, or be known for doing, good in a particular area of concern. Today, nonprofit boards are expanding and revising their composition in an effort to gain a larger perspective toward building healthier, more inclusive communities. Additionally, the work taken up by nonprofit boards span a larger terrain of the social concerns facing our society. The depth and scope of these issues require greater effort in an attempt to make a difference.

Many of these social issues spawn other concerns making the work more complex. For example, the numbers on homelessness are on the rise. As these numbers swell, so do they interrelate with other cultural and socioeconomic challenges. Consider that the rising cost of adequate housing for low and moderate-income households, affects health care, education, transportation, individual isolation, crime rates and so much more – all the kind of issues that nonprofit organizations strive to address.

The point is to acknowledge that as the business landscape and issues affecting communities evolve, so too must those of us who have a seat at decision-making tables of organizations. Presented here, is the idea that boards must evolve, shift, modify, and change how the work gets done while striving to remain relevant and engaged to those we aim to serve. In this changing climate, boards are being called into a time demanding adaptability, not by sacrificing governance, but opening anew to unprecedented opportunities to make a difference in transforming communities.

In *Boardroom Culture Shock*, I speak of culture shock in a good way. It is intended to demonstrate a trajectory toward needed changes regarding how boards can up-level their performance and increase their overall effectiveness on behalf of the organizations they serve. If you currently sit on a board, or have in the past, you know that while board service can be very rewarding, there can be challenges in the boardroom. Perhaps you were like me when I first discovered the type and level of dysfunction within some boards. I admit that there were times I was... shocked.

In *Boardroom Culture Shock* you'll find seven key strategies that can shift aspects of a board's culture that will strengthen board member engagement, competence and performance. In some cases, implementing even one of these strategies can transform the quality of the deliberations in the boardroom. I am like many others who work with boards in knowing that highly-functioning boards of directors, hold an important key to an organization's success. This is not to dismiss the value of "rubber stamp" boards or boards where members are placed to assure seats are filled, they have their place. However, in this book I'm extending an invitation to those who are willing to assess their board's current culture, in an effort to elevate the capacity of the decision-makers at the boardroom table.

As of this writing, I have facilitated many trainings, retreats, and what I call enrichment programs for boards. Noticing, again and again, certain counterproductive attitudes, I began to approach my work from a different angle. What I noticed is certain attitudes at their worst, set in motion the board's overall inability to work together effectively. I began to follow where certain behaviors and actions would lead. Sometimes they led to conflicts, firing of the CEO, board members leaving the board angry and hurt, the board fending itself against legal, ethical and financial problems. Yes, in my early days as an inexperienced board consultant, the behaviors shocked me. Most importantly, I noticed these behaviors were ingrained in the culture of the board and all too often led to the board being distracted from the mission, the vision, and the organizational values.

Fortunately, these counterproductive attitudes generally didn't all apply to a single board simultaneously. Here are the attitudes and behaviors I noticed that became obstacles to effective board functioning, and therefore a barrier to organizational health, growth, and sustainability. These counterproductive attitudes are also addressed by chapter in the order listed:

1. A subtle disconnect from the mission, vision, and organizational values.

2. Relationships were often barely tolerable with some members unengaged.

3. Difficulty accepting and addressing a need for change.

4. Blinders on regarding who's perspectives were missing from a seat at the table.

5. Clear and noticeable division between the CEO and the board.

6. Fragmented and divisive attitudes about money-related issues.

7. Soft positioning for growth by low attention to stewardship, exposure of assets to risk, and goodwill.

Where these behaviors and characteristics where present, they formed underlying factors that shaped the board's culture. Here's where the culture shock came into existence. The boards that were knee deep in any, or several, of these counterproductive attitudes were "shocked" to hear it. They were simply functioning the way they always had. They had not considered the level and depth of the barriers they had set in place stifling the board's overall effectiveness. It took having the observation of someone from outside the organization to thrust on them the idea of looking at the culture from a wider lens.

It leads us to this: traditions brought forward from previous board leadership must be reviewed from time to time. If not, we risk binding new boards to old ways and methods of board service – the good, the bad, and yes...the ugly. The tactics that worked at some point in the past may need reshaping for a board culture that is relevant for current times, current social issues and current constituents. Without renewing or upgrading the strategies that affect attitudes, behaviors, and the ways of doing things, boards today may find themselves locked into modes of conduct that challenge organization growth and sustainability.

The book I published before this one, *The Power of One Accord*, was my way of addressing the value of high-quality relationships on the board. That book takes board members from being tolerant of one another to learning to develop trust at the level of harnessing a working connection that is synergetic. It was also written with faith-based organizations in mind. In this book, we cover board relationships as part of just one of the themes affecting the board's overall culture.

Throughout the book, when I speak of the board, I am including the CEO unless otherwise noted. While not all CEO's are voting members of the board, they do have a seat and a voice at the boardroom table. It is my hope too, that the CEO and board strive to build a strong team, which requires all hands working together in order to lift the mission, enhance the vision and utilize the values of the organization for greater success and impact. Also, I use "board" referring to boards of directors as well as boards of trustees. Further, I refer to nonprofit organizations with the idea of including all types of organizations that are organized to focus on a cause, over profits. While some of the strategies here can be helpful to for-profit businesses, those with people first, cause first, will most likely realize the greatest benefit.

Each chapter:

- introduces one of the seven strategies that when addressed can shift the board toward greater competence and expand its capacity.
- lists a series of questions boards can use as discussion starters designed to strengthen the understanding of the ideas presented in the chapter.

- is finalized with a section to highlight the practical application of the chapter's subject.

It is my hope that giving attention to the core ideas presented, this book can assist boards in unleashing the hidden potential laying wait in the boardroom. With members who want to serve on a team of committed leaders, here is an opportunity to take board service and all the joys associated with striving toward a great cause to new levels of personal and professional heights.

If you've made it to this point, it means that you did not shy away from the title. And I'm going to assume that just maybe, you have a bit of a curious or adventurous spirit. So, if you're ready to raise the quality of your board's overall experience and impact, let us begin a journey through these pages to increase your board's capacity toward its next level of performance, effectiveness, and success.

Chapter 1

ANCHOR TO PURPOSE

"The meaning of life is to find your gift
the purpose of life is to give it away."

–William Shakespeare

y position on board service has evolved greatly over time. This chapter describes the beginning of my journey working with boards. It reveals the genesis of my commitment to helping them champion the cause to which they are dedicated to serving. It also describes our first culture shock, revealed when a board discovers and acknowledges it has become separated from that which anchors them to board service and the organization they serve.

Anchor, in this context, is a fastener, that which secures a thing in place. Liken this to an anchor that holds a ship in steady position when not at sea. When heavy winds and strong currents rise, the anchored ship will not drift away but stands firmly, securely in location. When it is time to set sail, the ship is a ready vessel for the captain and crew to implement the navigation plan that will guide the ship to its intended destination. The following story is one example of a board that has become separated from its anchor, that which holds it in place—the organization's purpose for being, and the board's purpose for serving.

The first board retreat I was asked to facilitate was over thirty-five years ago, as of this writing. I admit, I was not prepared for what ensued. The CEO, a young woman of a community-based nonprofit organization, contacted me saying, "My board has some issues we need to get out on the table and work through. Would you facilitate a retreat for us so we can get back on track with our purpose?" At that time, I had a naïve idea about what boards do or should do. Not having served on a board, I had a romanticized idea of how boards functioned. My area of expertise at that time was facilitating retreats, workshops, and seminars for individuals on various inspirational themes. I believed I was qualified for the task, and for whatever reason this young CEO trusted me. She had attended a workshop I had given on goal-setting and came to the idea I could help. I later discovered she had consultants working with the board prior to contacting me, and the situation had not improved.

The retreat was scheduled for a full weekend at a beautiful retreat center. I arrived early so that I could meet some of the board members as they arrived and have time with the CEO before our first session. The CEO appeared nervous as we spoke but, I didn't give it much thought. At that time, I did not know her job was on the line. As the board members arrived, they seemed pleasant enough, so I felt good going into our first activity, an icebreaker.

Generally, facilitators don't expect anything to go wrong during the icebreaker, but something did. All of the board members seemed willing to participate, except one. He was a man of tall stature, had a deep, commanding voice, and was clearly not interested in anything where he was not the center of attention. He even persuaded a few of the other ten board members not to participate. Did I mention that this was the ice-breaker?

He shook his fist saying, "This is a waste of time. There are pressing matters that we should be working on, not playing games." I had lost control of the room. I looked over at the CEO and immediately realized that something bigger was going on beyond her initial statement to me. Yes, looking back, I had not known the importance of doing a good front-end consultation with the CEO before agreeing to facilitate a retreat. I had walked into something for which I was ill prepared.

Without telling the whole story, let me just say that the ice-breaker moment was just the beginning to a weekend that ended with the CEO in tears after being bullied by this imposing structure of a man while the other board members watched. As I attempted to intervene, this man, with thunder in his voice, pointed at me saying, "You, shut up, this is none of your business!" I remember sitting there thinking, no, praying, that another board member would stand up for the CEO or at least stand up to this man and say something about his behavior.

It was appropriate for this board member to express his position of having a legitimate issue to address. However, what I was not prepared for was the way he exercised pure intimidation and harassment, and I was sure this was not the first time he had been so hostilely vocal. I left the retreat center on the third day feeling like I had been held captive in a nightmare. I remember saying to myself, "I'll never work with a board again."

It was months before I would sit down with pen and paper to form a list of lessons learned driven by my "curiosities" about that experience. The strongest curiosity resurfaced when I started to work with boards years later and even reoccurs in my mind every now and again. Why did ten people watch a single person on their board terrorize the CEO and not intervene? Why did they subject themselves to the rude, vicious performance of one man? Why were those board members serving on that board?

Years later, I had my own "nightmare" experience with my board as CEO. However, this time I did not end the experience as I had long ago saying, "I'll never work with a board again." Rather, this time I said, "I want to work with boards because I know there has to be a better way." Herein I have described what anchors me to my purpose for doing this work.

It is my hope that you will find what anchors you to the purpose behind which you have decided to serve on your board. And that the board will seek to anchor itself to the organization's cause, its purpose for being. That anchor should be a fastener that keeps board members and CEO alike focused on the mission, vision, and organizational values. Throughout the book when I reference the board, I am including the CEO unless I make a specific distinction. The seven strategies in the book effect all those seated around the boardroom table and that includes board members as well as CEO.

This work has been challenging and yet rewarding. Challenging because boardroom behavior is not always harmonious. Rewarding, when there is a glimpse of possibility, a flicker of a new insight, a flash of hope that makes itself known in the boardroom by one, two, or more board members.

It signals an awakening to the possibility that there is a better way to work together toward a good cause, absent of contention, conflict, and controversy. Yes, some of the behavior I've seen in boardrooms is just plain "bad." Perhaps you've experienced some of that too. But the reward comes when bad shifts to better, better moves toward good, and good just keeps evolving.

Many would agree that we have reached a critical mass where cultural, environmental, economic, and social issues are too large to ignore or kick down the road. Boards of today's nonprofit organizations have multiple layers of concerns facing them, many of which shake them to the core of their organization's sustainability. Systemic social, cultural, and economic tremors, that have for many years permeated our society, are now more rigorous and pronounced, causing boards to need effective functioning like never before. The affecting issues range from the rising cost of doing business, increased demand for the kinds of services nonprofits deliver, shifting demographics, globalization and the technological advances that cause major instability in job markets previously enjoyed.

So, nonprofit organizations of today need boards who are anchored to good causes with a big vision for the possibilities of what can be achieved. This ideal requires sound governance, members from diverse perspectives making decisions and policies, shared mutual respect and value among those seated in the boardroom, and a team approach between the board and CEO.

I'm hoping that board members that take up reading this book hold optimism for what an effective board can achieve. Perhaps you hold a measure of insight into the importance of uninhibited focus toward fulfillment of what I'll refer to as the organization's big three: mission, vision, and organizational values. I'm going for an attitude of high optimism for the organization's overall ability and capacity to address challenges implied or stated by the mission and vision. The intent here is to encourage those who are ripe for taking a significant cause to a new level by the giving of their gifts of time, talent and resources to bring their best to the boardroom.

While everyone belongs to or is connected to some organization that has a board of directors (or board of trustees), not all are willing to learn of the great responsibilities that come with it. From the school board, home owner's association, a religious or spiritual community, a nonprofit organization to a for-profit company the general population may know of "the board," but not understand the board's role. Boards are part of how we, as a society have configured the management of our affairs. Most organizations, businesses, and associations operate with a board as part of its structure. While we belong to these organizations that have some influence on so much of our daily lives, most of us know little about how they function. For most of us, unless we've had board experience or studied them, if asked to be on a board, few know what boards actually do, or should not do.

So, one key challenge is that many people join a board not having good knowledge of what is expected of them and how they can best fulfill the role of board member. Their heart may be in a good place for saying "yes," but this alone can prove to be problematic for the board member, board, and organization. When we find boards that are unsure, unclear, and under-performing, it should be no surprise that seated at the boardroom table we find good people that are uninformed of what is expected of them. Lack of clarity around who does what is very often a question on the mind of board members, even those who have served for a while often admit to not fully understanding their roles and responsibilities.

This chapter gives emphasis to the first of the seven strategies that have the potential to reshape the culture of the board toward greater competence and performance. Our discussion here is the fundamental anchor for boards that move the needle forward toward a greater impact in the communities they serve.

Early on from my facilitation of board trainings and retreats, I noticed that when the discussion was on the topics of strategic planning, fundraising, finances, or who's supposed to be doing what and isn't, we'd have a robust, lively discussion. But when I asked how they felt about the mission, even asking individual board members to talk about their connection to the mission the conversation was sparse, lacked passion and substance. In some discussions, the mission presented members with great differences in their understanding of the mission and what it strives to achieve. The group would desire to get back to the "issues that matter," meaning finance, the CEO's performance, growth, and long-term sustainability. They felt more comfortable with discussing these because the mission caused such divergent viewpoints that only a commitment to more time and energy could a collective understanding be reached.

Herein lies the concern or problem I raise. Yes, the organization's financial affairs, CEO's performance, growth, and long-term sustainability are important. However, all these rest on the mission as a foundation. After all, the mission tells the board what the organization stands for and gives the leadership the platform upon which to anchor. So, when meeting with a board that is uneasy or unclear in their discussion of the mission, my concern is that they are not anchored in the organization's real purpose. And while they may be very busy making decisions, policies, and resolutions, they may have subtly separated their deliberation discussions from the mission, vision, and organizational values. When those sitting at the decision-making head of the organization have little connection to, focus on, or concern for, the purpose of the organization, this tampers with the organization's capacity to grow and positions the board members themselves for ineffective performance as a board.

Boards make decisions. They hire the organization's leader, the CEO. They chart and enforce the direction of the organization. By way of financial oversight, strategic planning, and assuring legal compliances are met, boards have great license over the affairs of an organization. These are areas that fall under the heading of board governance; And, there's more. An organization that has a compelling purpose as revealed by its big three, deserves a board that is anchored in the purpose for which the organization exists. All the better if board members have a personal connection to the mission, vision, and organizational values.

The board holds a great power which is derived from its many responsibilities. If that power is not claimed and activated, it may become one of the core causes of conflict, organizational dysfunction, and set the stage for division among board members. This great power is the mission as the centerpiece for all that the organization does, the board's overall understanding of it, and the extent to which individual members connect with it. Additionally, this position is raised even higher when every member of the board has a distinction between what he or she is there to "do" and what they are there to "be."

While meeting the governance requirements assures the board is "doing" the right things to operate and function, it does not assure its success in fulfilling the organization's purpose, because that requires clarity around "being." Even if the board is meeting the prescribed duties around financial, legal, and strategic areas, this is no assurance of the organization's success in impacting its constituents or its long-term sustainability. These "doings" of certain duties that boards have, can be, and in many cases are, absent of the board owning the power that is inherent in a collective focus on a great mission and vision. Board members are to "be" advocates for the organization's work. The power of the board is in "being" a magnified force where members all align with a mission, vision and set of organizational values as champions for the cause. Each person contributes at a higher level when they are anchored to the organization's purpose and inspired by their individual and personal reasons for saying "yes" to board service.

In my work with boards, I ask the question, "What caused you to say "yes" to serve on the board of this organization?" There are two main ideas I'm getting at with this question; did you get them? I want to know why they are willing to utilize their time, talent and resources, first to serve on a board in general. Second, why this particular organization? Often the initial response is superficial. We may hear something like, "Well, these folks don't know what they're doing, and they need my help" (yes, that was a real response). Or, "This will look good on my resume" (another real response). However, I want the respondent to drill down deeper until we get at the core reason a person would use the precious commodities of time, their skills, talents, earned abilities, and financial resources, to sit in a meeting on whatever frequency the board convenes. I'm wanting this admission, not for me, but for the board members themselves. When we are conscious of our deeper reason for serving on the board, anchoring questions can help refocus the individual back to the greater motive for being there. With this awareness, members come to board meetings not just to sit, but to serve and "be" a positive force for the mission. From this state of awareness, those seated at the boardroom table are positioned to align their willingness to serve with such qualities of character like empathy, kindness, and optimism.

I once facilitated a workshop where one member of the board felt out of sync with the rest of the members of the board. He often took the opposing position on nearly every issue and had become what some thought of as a "troublemaker." His first responses to my question of why he said yes to serving on the board were superficial. But as he went deeper, it turned out someone close to him had passed away just before he came on the board and he was coping as best he could with grief. That distress often came out like an attitude of bitterness, indifference, and hostility that was projected toward fellow board members in general board discussions.

Drilling down on the anchoring questions, he got in touch with his connection to the mission. It was an organization that helps those who have lost a loved one. Although he had not taken up the services of the organization directly to work through his grief, he knew first-hand the importance of the work the organization did. I'm happy to report that this member had a turning point moment. His attitude shifted toward being more open and honest with fellow board members. And some board members actually befriended him after that and were there to support him during a very difficult time.

The revelation was not just for the one board member, who after that day was a better board member—committed to the mission, vision and values while lending his very valuable skills, talents and resources. But the whole board had a shift in how it related to each other, and the mission.

I asked the question, "Why did no one know this man had lost someone close to him?" Apparently, there was no real time for board members to get to know each other beyond a cordial greeting before board meetings. Over and over again, I've experienced that when a group of people gather for a very focused, fixed intention, it often leaves out the value of human connection and appreciation. As human beings, we are simply better together when we connect in positive ways and demonstrate even a minimal level of care for each other. So, when I'm talking with a board, I'm wanting to draw out their connection to the mission, vision, and values of the organization. I'm wanting to hear their desire to lift the mission so that change happens, improved quality of life happens, and something gets made better that will raise the standard of joy and equality for others.

I am also listening to and watching how they connect with each other. Human beings are social creatures, and it is simply an easier path to work with each other when we at least admit our need for human interaction, acknowledgement, and touch.

It has been my choice to focus on nonprofit and not-for-profit organizations because the work done under a mission that changes life for the better is done by so many of these organizations. This keeps me inspired and dreaming that board service will be an uplifting, meaningful act of service for causes that positively affect the lives of others.

The organization's vision and values generally strive to reflect the ideal of helping to make something better for those the organization attempts to serve. I dream too, that boards use their human power and potential to affect change by championing a mission that is transforming and a game changer in the quality of life for individuals, families, communities, neighborhoods, and the world. It is a lot easier to join together in accomplishing a great cause, if those who are working toward that goal can do so from harmonious relationships where there is mutual appreciation, trust, and respect.

This attitude toward board service can invite an approach toward striving higher as a team. In this way, ego driven personalities, that are so often distractors from the agenda and the mission, have a way of fading (sometimes by resignation). I'm not suggesting that the board be a great love fest with no disagreements. Even in the best marriages and relationships people disagree. But they work through it because they know the relationship matters in the grand scheme, the bigger picture of their lives.

Boards can benefit greatly from overcoming the single-pointed view of board service as governance that dictates checking the boxes of tasks and duties out of obligation and debt to be paid for sitting at the boardroom table. When a board revisits the common thread that weaves the mission, vision, and organizational values, they clarify their anchor—the organization's purpose for being and magnify the commonality which brings them together. Boards that are infused with a passion for the organization's purpose share momentum of hope and intention for accomplishing great things. In this way, the power of the unity of those seated on the board becomes a worthy investment of one's time, talent and personal financial resources.

The first of seven strategies to amplify the competence and capacity of board culture:

Board members anchored in the purpose for which the organization exists, position themselves as a compelling team to champion the mission, vision, and organizational values.

DISCUSSION STARTERS:

1. What caused you to say "yes" to serve on this particular board?

2. In your own words, describe what the mission means? Give examples of the mission at work.

3. Describe any experiences you've had, whether past or present, that support your understanding of the mission.

4. Describe how you believe the constituents of the organization directly benefit from the services the organization provides.

5. Name something the organization does that underscores the significance of the organization.

6. How do the mission, vision and organizational values connect to one another?

7. Give examples of how the board may continually hold the mission, vision, and values as the centerpiece in all that it does.

PRACTICAL APPLICATION:

Keep the mission, vision and organizational values visible, and alive in the minds and hearts of the members of the board. Find practices to do this in positive, creative, engaging, and fun ways. Here are a few to consider:

- Print them on the agenda of meetings.

- Recite them at the opening of meetings.

- Test them against new programs before approval. Ask, "How does this program align with our mission, vision, and values?"

- Take a few moments at some point in the meeting for a board member to share something that connects them to, highlights the importance of, the mission, vision or an organizational value. This can be current or from their past. Ask a different board member to share each meeting.

- Have a member share a "Current affairs moment." This is taking time to remind the board of the relevance of the organization's purpose by reporting something in current affairs that demonstrates the need for the organization and the value of the organizations big three. While sometimes current affairs as reported in the news can be negative, find the positive aspect of the story connecting with mission, vision or values.

Chapter 2

MIND-POWER IN THE BOARDROOM

A mind is a terrible thing to waste.

–Arthur Fletcher

Years ago, there was a television commercial for the United Negro College Fund that spoke the phrase coined by then CEO Arthur Fletcher, "A mind is a terrible thing to waste." The great achievements of humankind have come from ideas. An idea comes into manifest form when it is conceived, nourished with belief, strengthened with the energy of persistence, and birthed into existence. But the idea had its genesis in the mind. If just one mind can conceive of a worthy idea, then what is the potential for ideas spawned from a team of minds, joined together, focusing on a single cause? In this chapter, I describe our second culture shock. This is revealed when a board discovers that by failing to promote and allow time for generative sharing, they waste the potential for larger, more impactful ideas to evolve from the collective wisdom assembled in the boardroom.

The idea of using our minds intentionally as a collective group is not new. It is referred to by different names. One commonly used term for this in motivational and business circles today is the "mastermind" principle. The practice brings together a carefully selected group of individuals who join their thinking ability in a time of collective sharing, to contribute to the illumination and amplification of a specific topic. In this chapter, I use the term "mind-power." I'm referring to the collective, focus and intentional use of our mind abilities to draw forth creativity, from a group composed of a variety of backgrounds and wisdom of experience. It may also be a culture shock moment to admit that what makes this level of creative idea conception valuable is when there are trusting, mutually respectful relationships around the boardroom table that invite open and honest dialogue.

Looking around the boardroom table from a traditional lens, perhaps we have failed to notice or fully engage the rich resources lodged in the minds and hearts of those seated at this honored table of leadership. One challenge I've often noticed stems from those "mind" abilities going under-utilized, unnoticed, untapped, misdirected, or simply put—wasted. I'm not saying that lots of talking from individuals at the table has been absent. I am suggesting that there is a weak link in board deliberations and decision-making, that lies in under-utilizing the mind-power that could be engaged to shape rich, creative, innovative, generative discussion.

This chapter is about magnifying the mind-power assembled at the boardroom table to allow for a broader perspective of wisdom, experience, knowledge, and discernment by which to manage the affairs of the organization. When individuals who respect the wisdom of varied experience and knowledge, tap into their combined mental ability, they position themselves for a high-quality, magnified outcome. So, when the board reveres the value of mind-power and singly focuses on a shared purpose, ideas worthy of exploration will have fertile soil upon which to appear, and subsequently grow.

The ideal board of directors is one where those who have heard and answered the call to serve are fully available to contribute a wide range of skills, talents and expertise from diverse backgrounds, and experiences. They are placed in the position of shaping the health, growth, and sustainability of the organization. It follows that their collective and combined ideas have the potential to take the organization to its next level of progress.

In the boardroom, we fulfill the appropriate oversight required, but it can also be a place of joint mental exploration. Through dialogue, discussion, and discovery the boardroom table can be the place where we access channels of resources not previously examined. When the collective mind-ability of those seated at the boardroom table is tapped to advance the big three (mission, vision, organizational values), a new level of decision-making comes into being.

While we don't list board members on the organization's balance sheet under assets, the idea as a metaphor could have merit if we viewed the collective mind-power of the board, as a dividend producing stock. The rich ideas that can be generated from a carefully crafted team of committed individuals who champion the same mission is the stuff of which big things happen. Just think of it, rather than a "board meeting" as usual, perhaps the "convening of great minds" would be something to aspire to.

A BOARD CULTURE LACKING IN CAPTURING THE COMBINED WISDOM, CREATIVITY, AND VARIED MIND-POWER, NEGLECTS A THREE-FOLD OPPORTUNITY.

The first neglected opportunity is presented in a more concise and brief description than the two that will follow. This topic starts the conversation with failing to recognize the importance of forming relationships with those around the boardroom table. Relationship development serves to craft an environment upon which to build trust, mutual respect, and value. On large boards, this is a little more difficult to achieve, but important never the less.

Consider that when in a group setting, many find it easier to speak up and contribute to a conversation when they feel at least a basic level of safety in the group. Yes, often time we have extroverts and type A personalities who have no problems imparting their opinions. However, the outspoken ones are not the only people around the table who may have meaningful thoughts and ideas to share. Surely those who appear quiet were recruited for some good reason. So, the suggestion is to put time, energy, and effort into creating a board culture where everyone's voice matters. Set an intention toward building relationships among those who have a seat at the table. Upon those connections will rest the possibilities for a mix of fresh ideas with the potential to spawn narratives difficult to unveil when discussions lack trust, mutual respect, and value among those in the room.

The second neglected opportunity is downplaying the impact of idea sharing, creative dialogue, and brainstorming around the issues facing the organization. Herein, the board has an unwrapped gift sitting in the middle of the boardroom table. It's there. It's at every meeting.

Instinctively, we know that it will take time, effort, and patience to open the gift and begin the process of how it is best used and applied. But if we remain in the comfortable space of attempting to work from the knowledge of what we already know, we miss the opportunity to learn something that could enhance our experience. It reminds me of my early days of owning my first cell. I'd had it for some time and my son, then a teenager, worked diligently to convince me it was time for an upgrade. The fact that I had a cell phone was fine with me. Although basic in features, I was content with it. My son attempted to prove to me there was so much more I could do with a simple upgrade. I didn't want to expend the mental energy to learn of the latest features, when new technology was clearly traveling far ahead of my skill level. Yes, I could see that an upgrade might have value, but it looked to be more work in learning how to operate it than I wanted to expend in time, and mental energy. I fought it for as long as I could.

Finally, three iterations later, I gave in to an upgrade. I had been right. It took mental energy and repeated effort for me to learn how to operate my new phone that could do more than I ever imagined I'd ever need. Once I learned how to access the new features, I wondered how I had ever lived without them. Funny though, afterward, all of those "fancy" features soon became second nature and more like necessities to my lifestyle. The point in all of this, is that I labored in a level of comfort that allowed me to avoid something easily available and directly beneficial, because I concerned myself with the time and energy it would take to learn how to use what turned out to be a gift.

Now, I do understand that it takes time to go into dialogue mode in a board meeting, especially in an unstructured format. So, I say, structure the format. Plan specific times for open dialogue and create what will work for the board members and the subject matter. One of the common complaints I hear is that board meetings are "boring and too long." Perhaps these are the meetings that could use re-structuring.

We want to avoid the situation where a long agenda becomes the prohibitor of allowing conversation around issues that are important only to discover that we have spent more time on issues that are of lesser significance. Surely, we want to finish the meeting in a timely matter, so everyone can go about their wonderful, important, busy lives. Now, I'm all for living a wonderful, important, and busy life. However, when it is seen as something separate from the wonderful, important, and commanding work we apply to fulfill a mission that has the potential to change lives, we have let a precious event slip through our hands. In this circumstance, board meetings can become something members do to plow through the agenda on some form of autopilot. In this way, we have "wasted" an opportunity for our mind-power to address and solve issues before the board, or to tap into fresh new strategies that will grow the organization.

I once met with a board for a training session and they shared how proud they were because their board meetings were one hour. They repeated, "We have a one-hour board meeting, once a month."

When I did not give a big congratulatory response, one of the board members persisted.

"I'll bet you don't see that very often?"

"Yes. You are correct," I said.

Still not satisfied with my reaction, another board member continued, "We've worked very hard to structure our meetings, so we get in, get the business done, and we're all on our way. But you don't seem to be very impressed," the member exclaimed.

The board chair immediately chimed in, "We're all extremely busy people so we decided that our board meetings would be short and concise."

We had just completed a discussion that revealed several items that the board needed to address and had not done so. The work done between board meetings and in committees also revealed that even more items had simply not been completed in a timely matter. Now, here is where I had to choose my words very carefully but speak to an important observation. I said, "The length of the board meeting should be secondary to the quality of discussion, decisions you make, and dialogue that advances your mission, vision, and organizational values." I didn't want to totally squash their efforts, but it needed to be said. As we looked at some of the challenges facing the organization, I could see that the length of board meetings had evolved into a greater priority than using their time together to generate solutions by accessing and using the mind-power assembled on the board, and actually addressing key issues. It was not a matter of commitment, they had simply gotten off track.

I wanted them to know there was another way to do board meetings, and board service that can support the intent and purpose for which board members choose to serve. Coming together for the board meeting does not have to be like taking a bitter pill. The work can be done and still be respectful of board members' time.

Additionally, board service can and should be something that is meaningful and fulfilling. It should add to that intrinsic feeling most people who join a nonprofit board have - they want to make a difference. Even if it is in some small way, they are committed enough to willingly apply whatever skills, talents, and abilities they have to embrace the hope of contributing to a worthy cause. Most people find enjoyment in giving of themselves and serving toward the fulfillment of something they have deemed worthwhile. So, when the board meeting is described as boring, something else is going on.

Board meetings are generally thought to be boring when:

- they are unproductive - that is, nothing transpires that contributes to the forward movement of the big three,

- during the meetings an individual dis-engages, feeling there is little or no recognition of their presence or appreciation of their contribution,

- there is a lack of trust and mutual respect among board members,

- there are one or more board members who seem to dominate every meeting,

- the board members around the table seem to have lost sight of the significance of the mission, the inspiration of the vision and a dedication to the organizational values,

- the meeting is so loosely structured it poses as dysfunction or gross disorganization.

Notice that most of the factors affecting boring meetings have to do with relationships. The relationships around the boardroom table can greatly support the ability to work together as a team or become the catalyst for members to shut down and withhold that which may well contribute to the solving of the issues on the table. Generative dialogue can be healthy and very productive. However, in order for creative sharing time to be effective, there must be trust and mutual respect. This is built over time and with intention. What happens far too often, though, is that boards attempt to "do the business" of the organization as individuals rather than as a team working together toward a common purpose. All too often board members find themselves barely tolerating each other, not because they are "unpleasant or unkind" people but rather because relationships have not been developed.

When relationship building is absent from the culture, we will have some board members who are present at the meeting, but not engaged in the affairs. Here, the organization suffers, and so do the individual board members who agreed to serve because they wanted to contribute and make a difference.

When relationships on the board are barely tolerable, the joy of board service is sorely lacking. In this environment, attempts at open dialogue often lead to harsh words, and words spoken harshly. Of course, when this is the case, the energy in the boardroom reeks of indifference. Egos take center stage. The items on the agenda receive less than the best from the members. Common civility yields to the loudest voice, or to those personalities auditioning for who's right by pointing out who's wrong. No trust. No harmony. Not an avenue for good decision making. If board meetings follow this track, then of course this is a case for short board meetings. The mind-power at the boardroom table can be one of our greatest resources, but again, this power must be invited and used.

The third and final neglected opportunity occurs when we fail to carefully craft the make-up of those seated at the boardroom table so that there are a variety of perspectives, backgrounds and expertise represented to add quality and richness to boardroom deliberations. From the position of crafting a competent board, the subject of compiling a diverse group of members has a definite place in our discussion here and is one that should be on the table for discussion in the boardroom.

Crafting a diverse board where everyone is included, valued and acknowledged is a subject that deserves more time than we shall address in this chapter. There are many books that address the subject well as it relates to why it is culturally, socially, and economically important. For now, let us acknowledge that there is value in the recognition of human differences sculpted by race, culture, age, gender, gender identity, ability, and socio-economic status, and that the organization is worthy of working toward this kind of leadership representation.

This chapter promotes the magnification of the mind-power of those seated at the boardroom table. So far, we've talked about having the necessary skills, talents, experience, and expertise required for the type of organizational structure we have, and that we aspire to build. Now we advance the discussion to include social, cultural and economic viewpoints that can demonstrate an appreciation for a diverse mix of "mind-power" at the table. The extent to which the board values a variety of perspectives in the boardroom will shape the quality, depth, and efficacy of creative, constructive, generative thinking.

The goal is to have a variety of voices at the table that are relevant to how we can best approach our mission, vision, and organizational values, in a changing world. This level of blending experience, expertise and backgrounds allows generative dialogue that can be highly informative and elevate creativity and innovation to new levels. When there are diverse perspectives backed by members who are inspired and connected to the mission and vision, the board has set in place a foundation that lends even greater value to the mind-power in board deliberations.

Boards are often challenged with shaping a diverse group of members. Recognizing the significance of a diverse board is one thing, taking the all-important steps of doing something about it is yet another. The "something" that must be addressed is crafting a board from the intent of having a variety of viewpoints across a range of individual life experiences and backgrounds that will contribute to decision-making and needed insight into short and long-term strategic direction.

Boards are generally better at intentionally building its makeup through the gateway of specific skill-sets and certain kinds of expertise. However, when the skill-set and expertise fail to reach further into areas where elements of social, cultural, and economic diversity are factored, the board narrows the possibility for a broader view on issues that may come before it. In this case, the parameters around the mind-power shared will have points of view limited to the narrow make-up of those who have a voice at the table. While a narrow range of opinions and perspectives may justify the board in making important decisions in silos, it may well leave board members ill-informed on issues, and ignorant of "unintended" consequences. Herein, the board will have a weak stand upon which to reach decisions for a wider constituent base, and risk miscalculation and incongruence with some aspect of the big three.

The board that intentionally designs its composition situates itself for the broadest range of possibilities, potential outcomes, and ideas that can spawn fresh approaches to organizational progress. When there is little or no diversity, the board risks the appearance represented by the surface view of optics, implying different viewpoints may not be valued as part of the board's organizational strategic trajectory. Herein, the board may find itself disadvantaged by ignoring the changing demographics of our times that tell us diversity not only has value now but will represent factors that affect sustainability going forward.

Having diversity in the boardroom can expand the mind-power by:

- Filling blind spots reflected by race, culture, age, gender, gender identity, ability, and socio-economic status;

- Bringing a unique stream of thought represented by life experiences different from those generally offered a seat at the table;

- Offering access to groups of people that may open networks beyond the board's reach;

- Providing reminders of issues and topics not regularly or naturally visited;

- Assuring the board is congruent with diversity and inclusion stated or implied by the mission, vision, and organizational values;

- Giving access to a larger constituent base, community, neighborhood, and global view;

- Supporting the board in remaining relevant in issues affected by increasing technological advances, shifting demographics and elevated social concerns.

If we can think of diversity as a resource that can support the process to achieve our big three, rather than an obligation to meet legal compliances or what addresses our optics, we will gain the greater benefits a wider viewpoint can yield. If a board wants to be relevant during the shifts in demographics and address the socially based issues of our time, it will take being responsive to and the inclusion of, a variety of voices on the board, executive leadership and staffing levels of our organizations.

A diverse board has the additional effort of insuring that every member of the group has a fair and equal opportunity to participate in all levels of the work, factoring-in their uniqueness. It means going the extra mile to assure every voice at the table is heard, valued and respected. A variety of perspectives will make for rich, thought-provoking, creative discussion that supports the personal and professional growth of each board member and aids the expansion of ideas for the board as a whole.

Finally, in the diversity, equity, and inclusion work being done at this point in time, over and over again we see statistics that reveal so many reasons why now, is a great time to move away from decision making in what often looks like closed associations. In a demonstration that the board is willing to reshape its culture around diversity, it can open the boardroom doors, change the seating to a round design, rearrange the social, cultural, gender and racial composition. Boards may well decide to take the opportunity to launch an effort that opens the way for unheard voices to be heard, add inclusive language, and place increased value on the quality of the mind-power at a diversified table. This may well be a culture shock undertaking; however, the benefits may well take the organization to a level not previously accessible.

The second of seven strategies to amplify the competence and capacity of board culture:

Board competence takes an upward progressive shift when it draws forth its mind-power from a diverse board representing a wide range of perspectives and backgrounds, enhanced by a culture of trust, mutual respect and appreciation.

DISCUSSION STARTERS:

- Discuss the idea of "mind-power" as an asset on the board and for the organization.

- Does the board have a team spirit backed by relationships that demonstrate mutual respect, trust, and appreciation for each other's service and contribution?

- Discuss the risks and rewards of creating a board culture of dialogue, sharing, creative discussion.

- In the normal course of deliberations discuss the extent to which everyone has an opportunity to give their input, and does?

- What is the level of variety of backgrounds and perspectives derived from racial, sexual orientation, age, culture, ability, and socio-economic differences on the current board? Discuss the board's responsibility and general position around operating from a diverse group of members as it aligns to the vision, mission and organizational values.

- By optics, would the constituents or the community at large determine that diverse perspectives matter as an organizational value?

- Does the board composition include a wide range of perspectives including those who are most affected by the fulfillment of the mission? Whose perspectives or voices are missing?

PRACTICAL APPLICATION:

Set aside time with the appropriate level of regularity that suits the board to:

1. Build relationships among those in the boardroom. This could be done by providing time for a brief check-in before delving into the agenda. Having a brief "social mixer" before board meetings. Assign "friend-development" pairs or groups that rotate each

month. Here, the board members would simply make it a point to connect with their assigned partner (s) once a week for a month. This could be for a brief phone call for a check-in, or meeting for a cup of coffee, etc. The point is to build and develop solid working relationships.

2. Decide on the best time and structure for generative discussion and dialogue sessions. Perhaps these will work best as a half-hour before or after each meeting, a special meeting, quarterly gathering or at an annual retreat. Again, large boards may work better in small groups.

3. To help maintain rich, high-quality discussions on issues facing the board, test the diversity of mind-power by regularly asking, "Whose perspective is missing from this discussion?" This is a way to continually monitor board composition. This may also serve as a reminder of candidate composition during the time of recruitment and provide topics of discussion for ongoing education.

Chapter 3

LISTEN TO THE VOICE OF CHANGE

When the winds of change blow, some people build walls and others build windmills.

–Chinese proverb

The winds of change are blowing with a fierce energy and it doesn't look as though it will be stopping any time soon. While the mission may seem to hold steady, we find that those we attempt to serve as a demographic are shifting as part of a fast-changing world. In this chapter, we describe our third culture shock. This is unveiled when a board discovers it has been a bit delinquent in recognizing and acting on signals calling for flexible or adaptive approaches to decision-making deliberations and strategic direction.

Just think of the archer's bow and how important is the precision of the aim. However, when the target keeps moving there is often a hit or miss outcome. This is how it may seem to organizations, businesses, and associations of our time; we have a mission, we aim, but the target is on the move. With the evolving success strategies for today's businesses in mind, the social and cultural shifting of demographics, increased social and socioeconomic issues, ever-changing laws and regulations, erratic political postures and technological advances that seem to be changing at the speed of light, how can a board keep up?

The boards of former days had a little more time on their side. Technological changes now give immediate access to data that in times past took several weeks or longer to gather and analyze. There was a bit more time for the CEO and staff to propose new ideas and projects. The slower methods of getting the data gave time to test the ideas, submit a report back to the board and allow a process of momentum to build over a longer period. But with data so readily and easily available, innovation has stepped up her game and implementation must move with her.

In former days, the goals in a strategic plan were made to stretch over a longer range of time. Today, it seems that time is of the essence on most things we do, lest we find ourselves obsolete and behind the times before we can even roll out a new program. Today, many nonprofit boards simply do not have the resources to implement what the available data suggests at the rate of speed of for-profit companies. It may be a culture shock moment to the board when it discovers that in addition to working on fine-tuning programs they are already behind and must struggle to catch up with new trends and initiatives. Boards may be stuck in a way of thinking that stems from days when the world of technology, information, and societal shifts did not spin around at a rate of greater speed than ever before.

Today, boards must shift toward being more adaptable, often not with time on their side. Strategies for moving the organization forward must strive with greater urgency to approach change viewing it on the horizon, rather than on the sunset of an innovative wave. With all the data available to anyone by way of our modern technological advancements, we can see the trajectory of what's shifting, changing, moving, coming our way from a distance if we are on the look-out. Of course, we could wait until the forecast has launched and passed. But then change is forced upon us and we are not prepared to give our best without needed preparation. An attitude that leans toward adaptability in strategic thinking and planning is required if we intend to progress toward our organizational vision and set in motion some degree of sustainability.

I was facilitating a board training some time ago and the question was raised from the floor, "We have great programs, but people don't seem to be responding, what should we do?" My response was,

- "Who says your programs are great?"
- "Who was in on the design and development of those programs?"
- "When did you last update your programs to assure they meet the needs of your current constituents?"

The conversation went longer than I had scheduled, as some of the participants took the questions personally. They took the path of thinking I was suggesting they were not doing a good work. It was, and is, no doubt in my mind that the many nonprofit organizations of our time really care, and work diligently to serve their constituents, communities, and causes that can make a difference in the quality of life for many. However, often the board working with the CEO has a strategic plan that does not get the "end users" direct feedback on the programs. So, the decisions sound very good on a board level and perhaps also on the senior staff level. But when the board is out of touch with looming changes affecting their industry, social and cultural shifts, their constituents, and the services offered, there may be a wide gap between who says it's a good program, and if it really meets the needs of current constituents.

When constituents aren't responding to the programs being offered all kinds of bells and whistles should go off. The programs that may have once been appropriate for clients of a former time may simply be out of date with those of the current demographic. Those programs may have been great for a former iteration of the client and customer base, but as we have said, times are changing rapidly and that means what people need, want and desire is shifting also.

For example, the current data tells us that the cultural and social shifts taking place now will continue in a direction of shifting the structure and ideal of what constitutes a family. The idea of family is no longer basic but a more complex entity to define, thereby causing change in what they need and want. Expanded beyond, one man, one woman, and two children, all of the same race, culture and religion is no longer the standard family norm in many communities. Surely this is the case for some, but there are many versions of family structures with many combinations for joining people together under the banner of family, household, neighborhood, and community. The dynamics of the changing family is re-sculpting neighborhoods and communities that were once stable in how they defined themselves and the trajectory of their growth. These same communities are faced with and challenged by, many uncertainties.

Now, you may not like where things are going, so your organization may attempt to keep things the way they were by failing to re-structure programs and services to meet the shifts now taking place. Yes, your organization could ignore the all-important assortment of changes. However, it would be at the risk of stifling to your organization's sustainability, progress and ability to be of service in this changing environment.

Starting with the people we aim to serve, boards should ask a few hard questions. The kinds of questions that force difficult conversations.

- Who do we aim to serve?
- Are we currently serving their wants and their needs? How do we know?
- What can we do to assure we are providing the right services to our intended demographic?
- Are we limiting the organization's potential by refusing to shift our strategies?
- Are we willing to adapt our thinking and strategies to adequately respond to the answers of the above questions?

Every organization, business, and association at this juncture in our human evolution must take its temperature and make a diagnosis regarding its willingness to change. That is, if it plans to be around for times to come. We must examine our mission statements, the vision we hold for the future, and our organizational values to determine if they are due an upgrade or an all-out restructuring. If our big three are intact for our cause, then we'll need to go to the next level of progression or the areas in many organizations that are now begging for reform. Again, do board members really understand the services provided by way of direct knowledge and exposure to the organization's constituents? The discussion among the board regarding the organization's programs may sound very different behind the closed doors of the boardroom than from the constituents at the location where they receive the services provided.

One Chinese proverb says, "When the winds of change blow, some people build walls and others build windmills." This provides a lot of food for thought. The winds of change should be a signal to organizational leaders to look more closely at the coming trends. The beauty of all the change we face is that much of it can be tracked and traced by our modern technological advancements. We have access to many "smart" ways of doing things. We have smartphones, smart televisions, smart security systems, S.M.A.R.T. strategies for meeting goals, the point is "smart" is no longer the issue for the average organization.

Think of it, when you decide you want to make a purchase, you simply turn on your phone or computer and within seconds you'll have the item on screen with price and delivery date. If your credit card is stored there, one click concludes the purchase – all in less than a minute. The winds of change have placed us in unparalleled times when we have but to Google almost anything we want to know, and we can have an answer in seconds.

Our challenge may not be one of are we smart enough but rather, are we asking the right questions and of the right people. When we do collect the data from our questioning process, are we willing to make corresponding changes to reflect our findings? Boards would do well to listen to what I think of as the voice of the changing winds. Let me illustrate this with a story.

When I lived in Miami, one of the things we experienced every year from June to December was hurricane season. Having grown up in the north, I was not familiar with the do's and the don'ts when a hurricane was headed our way. It took me several years to learn to take the matter seriously with appropriate action. One year we had been told to prepare for a hurricane that would be a level two or level three. My son, a teenager at the time, took it seriously and since we didn't have shutters, he decided to take the offer of a neighbor and stay at their home that was well secured for the level of storm anticipated. I, on the other hand, decided to stay home alone in our loosely prepared structure believing that the storm would not be so severe.

I had a minimal amount of concern until about 1:00 a.m., when the electricity went out and the sound of the wind startled me. The howling of the wind on that night, for a time, sounded like a train running through the neighborhood at a high speed. At that moment I heard what sounded like the loudest sound I'd ever heard. Then came the sound like muffled words of a deep voice. I did not discern specific words, but at that moment I remember coming to the belief that the wind, when it is fast enough, strong enough, fierce enough it has an audible sound like that of a human voice. The undiscerning voice of the wind had been clear enough to lead me to take hurricanes a lot more serious from that time forward.

When strong winds blow, like indicators and trends, I believe there is a message of change we should pay attention to. We may be tempted to downplay that the message is real particularly, if we don't have a metaphor of change where the wind moves things from one place to another – ready or not. The wind signals change is coming our way. Our approach may be to brace ourselves, so we don't have to move from where we are. We could dig in. Stay put. Stay our current course. But I dare ask, have you ever seen the effects of a tornado or hurricane? Did you see how the wind swept everything in its path to a new place. Buildings, people, cars, homes all moved from one place to another by strong force. We can fight the strong gusts of winds that tell us it may be time to change. Or, we can begin to look at the strong force of the wind as an opportunity to build momentum behind some of the areas where change is imminent.

What if we position ourselves to let the wind carry us onward? By resisting our own temptation to keep things the way they are, we could begin to see the wind as an ally to help us move from where we are to a place where we will have new opportunities we had not previously imagined.

Yes, some people build walls, these walls may be effective for a time, and perhaps that is what we believe is our best decision. But if the wind forces its way through a crack in a wall, the devastation can be more than we are prepared to handle. So, what about building windmills? The windmill moves with the wind. It uses the force of the wind to generate energy and power. If we are facing the winds of change perhaps we can make a conscious decision to use the change to create new ideas for improved services and programs that will have a greater impact on the mission, move us closer to the vision and still be a force for good with our values. Herein, boards will want to stay on the look-out for indicators and trends that will surely come as with the winds of change.

The third of seven strategies to amplify the competence and capacity of board culture:

Boards that adopt a practice of listening to change indicators position themselves for the flexibility to assume new pathways as an opportunity toward greater impact of the organization's mission.

DISCUSSION STARTERS:

1. Describe how the need for change on the board has been handled in the past.

2. What does the data reveal regarding current trends in your industry? Are there signs that indicate change is on the horizon that will affect your organization? What are they?

3. When did the board last get solid data regarding constituents, who they are and what they want and need?

4. What social, cultural, economic and technological changes are on the horizon that will affect what the board does and how?

5. What is the process when a shift in strategic direction for the organization is needed?

6. What can the board do to get in front of some of the changes that are trending that will affect the organization?

7. What can the board do to assure its ongoing openness to change and its willingness to evolve and grow?

Practical Application: Craft an ongoing practice for ways and methods of looking at new ideas for the future. Scheduling ongoing education, accompanied by time for generative discussion regarding industry trends, demographics, social, cultural and economic predictions, and forecasts can be helpful in broadening the minds and hearts of board members while cultivating their openness to change. Open-mindedness can be a great asset when the time comes to roll-out a major change in the organization.

Chapter 4

THINK BEYOND
THE NUMBERS

**Everything that can be counted does not
necessarily count; everything that counts
cannot necessarily be counted.**

–Albert Einstein

In business, numbers are an important tool by which we
measure the work that we do. As a tool the numbers can
help tell the stories behind why we do what we do, and
how we're doing in the process. However, there is a great need
to be conscious that numbers can be misleading in various
aspects of organizational affairs. This chapter describes our
fourth culture shock, revealed when a board comes face to face
with the realization that too often they allow numbers to tell
the narrative from which they operate. It is a culture shock
moment when realizing numbers tell only part of a story, often
missing the most important aspect of the story – people. It
brings to light that in order to tell the full story, the board may
need to understand the numbers and then, think beyond them.

For example, the numbers of a for-profit business may
render a very different narrative than the numbers of a

nonprofit. While both types of businesses need people and money to operate and grow, the order of priority is generally different. The for-profit business proudly posts its sign in any community, and it may read "Millions Served." To the for-profit business, this means that business is great, the money is flowing, shareholders are happy, and there is an indication that many satisfied customers bought their product.

However, if the nonprofit posts a sign of numbers served, those numbers would not be attached to dollars, although the organization may have indeed served millions. Imagine a sign on a homeless shelter "Millions Served." This would remind the public that the neighborhood has many people who don't have a place to live and may cast a negative shadow on that community. While those who work there are certainly happy to offer the services needed, at the same time, compassion may stir concern that so many people need those services. Depending on the type of organization, the social impact may be the deciding factor for the numbers to go down rather than up.

Nonprofit organizations generally have a purpose to have the number of people in society who need their help to go down over time by way of the work the organization provides. These organizations seek to reduce the number of people who are homeless, who are in need of affordable housing or who lack health care, and so on. So, a for-profit business and a nonprofit sign revealing the numbers "Served," tell two very different stories.

However, those numbers carry great power as they become the bases for determining how the organization plans to go forward. It may be a culture shock moment for the board, though, to realize how a narrative focused on numbers can be incomplete and thereby become a hindrance to innovative or creative solutions in its decision-making process.

Nonprofits have a structure that puts people first. They have the challenge of using one set of numbers to indicate the number of people who need their services, and another set of numbers as the dollars needed to be effective in their cause. It is important to use numbers with specific objectives in mind and present them to tell a specific portion of a story or chronicle certain actions. For example, when asking for funds as on grant applications, donor request letters, and reports to foundations, numbers may be used to demonstrate the value of specific programs indicating the capacity to serve large numbers of constituents, but also to make the case for funds requested.

While many organizational missions intend for the number of people needing services to go down, the organization generally will be asking for funding to go up. To keep pace with changing times and to present new and improved methods and programs, more money is required while decreasing numbers are served. The challenge today is the numbers often take on a very present burden. Higher numbers may indicate more people who are in need of services, while there may be less funds available to do the work. Stuck in this dilemma, the board, CEO, and staff must make a conscious effort to keep their own balance with the narrative shown by the numbers. Here they must work at managing the oscillation between ways to make the numbers work – big numbers in some places, smaller numbers in others.

The challenge for these decision makers is that they must remain conscious of the many methods in which numbers are used, for what purpose, and then determine how they best make the case for substantiating the narrative that supports the mission, vision and organizational values. It is all too easy when staring at numbers on pages to lose sight of the awareness that there are people behind those numbers who need the help the organization offers. Conscious attention must be paid to the value, purpose, and intent of the numbers presented. In fact, it will take sincere effort to be in dialogue regarding numbers in a report, behind the closed doors of the boardroom and yet, remember that the numbers reflect real people, with real challenges seeking real help for their lives. If the board loses sight of the people aspect of the organization's purpose, we fall into "numbers on a page thinking." This kind of limited thinking can foster dialogues that stifle growth and creativity around the boardroom table. Let me tell of a story that illustrates my position on this.

Some years ago, when I was a pastor of a church, a woman in our congregation had written an entire curriculum for an eight-week summer camp that we were blessed to receive a healthy grant for. The grant allowed us to offer the camp for "free" to children in the community where we were located. Of course, as with any grant, there were lots of guidelines by which we had to abide in order to maintain our funding, but we did the work. We also had many, many challenges that go along with having a "free" eight-week summer camp for kids five through twelve. There were challenges we anticipated and many we did not. But for several years we persevered because we knew the value it brought to the children and their parents and because we had funding from the grant.

We had a real opportunity to live our mission and make a difference in the lives of the children we served and in the surrounding community. However, if you've ever received a grant, you may have experienced the day when the grantor decides to "go in a different direction." In our case, this meant we would be expected to increase the number of children served on a lot less funding. So, the board deliberated and made the decision that without the grant the summer camp would not continue the following year. The camp staff and I were disappointed, but none of us could come up with ideas for alternative funding.

Several of the children who had been part of the camp were members of the congregation. So, when we announced that the summer camp would not be returning the following year, an eight-year-old girl who had been in the camp for the three previous summers came to me one Sunday after church. "Reverend Charline, why are we not having the summer camp?"

I attempted to explain, "Our funding will not be renewed next year."

With a puzzled look, she flung her hands wide, saying, "So why aren't we having the camp?"

Realizing I was going to need to give her more information, I said, "Well, it costs money to put on a summer camp and without the grant, we just don't have the funds to do it."

Now I thought I had explained this clearly enough, but when she came back the following Sunday and the Sunday after that for about six Sundays in a row, asking the question as though she had never asked it before, or as if I'd never attempted to answer.

I am embarrassed to say that it got to the point if I saw her coming to me on a Sunday I felt a bit nervous, because each time I looked at her cute and very sincere face I wanted to do something, but my response seemed to disappoint her more and more each week. I was actually having trouble sleeping and would see this little girl in my dreams.

After this had gone on for a couple of months, once again she came up to me, "Reverend Charline, why are we not having the summer camp?"

I had finally reached a moment where I could no longer give her my standard answer and I heard myself say, "Let me see what I can do."

At the next board meeting, I said to the board, "We have to find a way to have the summer camp." I told them about the little girl. It turns out she had approached a few of them as well. We decided to all join our "mind-power" together so we could explore ways that would allow us to have the camp. We did. Of course, the camp changed form, but there was indeed a camp the following year. The little girl who would not give up was our champion and spokesperson for the benefits of the camp.

I had to ask myself afterward, though, why it took the consistent inquiry of a child to force me and the board to look deeper. What made the difference? It was looking into the face of someone who was greatly affected by a decision we had made from the "numbers." The numbers told us we couldn't provide the services of the summer camp. However, looking into the face of a real live person, made the numbers only part of the equation and forced those at the decision-making table to factor in the compassion we felt for a little girl who wouldn't take no for an answer.

The camp had become an annual activity for one hundred children for several years. We at the boardroom table were removed from the personal value the camp provided. Yes, at the end of each camp cycle we had evaluations completed. But that produced another piece of paper with numbers on it that summarized the feedback. And, the numbers on the page had given us what we believed to be sufficient feedback over the years. Children loved it, parents loved it, and it was good for the community. We were serving our mission. Still, we surrendered to the numbers on the financial projection reports provided by the grantor and our own financial reports. We were willing to cancel the camp without delving into possibilities for living an important part of our mission, vision and organizational values. From behind closed doors of the boardroom, we had failed to think beyond the numbers.

Out of curiosity, I began to think back over some of the programs we had canceled over the years. Had we made those decisions staring at numbers? I had to think back, had we sought to engage in creative dialogue for new solutions? Did we attempt to build partnerships with other organizations? Had we invited suggestions and input from others? Did we consider collaboration as an avenue for providing what people needed? After many negative responses I found myself creating an affirmation for myself that I use even to this day: "Think beyond the numbers!" The gift given to our board was an opportunity to look at how we were governing. We all felt called to serve on the board because we had a love and concern for people, the mission, vision and organizational values. Yet at some point, we had stopped looking at people, closed ourselves off in the boardroom and made decisions based on numbers.

What I know now is if we just sit in the boardroom we will miss how important our decisions are to our constituents and fail to know their impact. We will lose the value gained by looking into the faces of those who want and need what the organization aspires to provide. If we can look them eye to eye and say, we've tried everything we can, we might determine we haven't. If we decide without input, feedback from our constituents, our method of deliberations will be incomplete. Until we humanize those who will be affected by our decisions, our job is only partly done. Too often boards make life-affecting decisions about numbers, rather than people. Many times, board members have not actually seen, or talked to the constituents that the mission, vision, and values attempt to lift-up and uphold. Yes, arriving at decisions may take a bit longer, but we gain the assurance that we honor those who may have something of value to add.

When we put effort into addressing some of the cultural, social and economic issues facing us today, let us get out of the boardroom for a while. Reading the reports have their place. For some boards, this will be a culture shock moment to shift beyond the "Numbers on a page thinking." Of course, we'll always have the financial reports and we shall be fiscally accountable. With on-going education for the board to increase their understanding of what the numbers reveal, thinking beyond the numbers can become a valuable shift in decision-making.

Until we give ourselves permission to expand our thinking by adding the human touch, putting a face and a heart with the issues on the agenda, we have not thoroughly explored all solutions or positioned ourselves to create new ones. Numbers will surely continue to be an important part of the narrative to be considered in board decisions. But let us also allow them to be a catalyst for reshaping the culture of the board encouraging every now and again to take a field trip, meet constituents face to face, hear their stories. We can access greater wisdom and creativity if we are willing to search beyond the numbers for that aspect of the story the numbers cannot reveal.

The fourth of seven strategies to amplify the competence and capacity of board culture:

The board can invigorate the decision-making process with fresh perspectives by a practice of thinking beyond the numbers and gathering input from a wider range of people.

Discussion Starters:

1. How does the board balance its focus between people and money?

2. Has there been an effort to build partnerships and collaborations with other organizations when numbers indicate a need to reach beyond available resources? What was the result?

3. Since being on the board what have you learned about the people the organization serves?

4. Do any board members fall into the category of constituents of the organization's services? If not, why? If yes, discuss the rationale of this decision.

5. Make a list of ways the board could get to know the people served by the organization.

6. What are some of the ways the board gets to experience the mission in action?

7. Describe benefits that may arise from making a connection to the organization's constituents?

Practical Application:

Schedule some real face time with those that the organization serves. It can be an event that allows the board members to get to know people and that allows people to get to know the board members. Caution: Do not plan this from the silo of the boardroom. Avoid the temptation, "We know a great event we can put on in order to meet the people." Allow the constituents to participate in the planning of the event. In one instance, an organization planned a celebration dinner at a nice hall for constituents away from the community where most of them lived. The board's thinking was that it would be good for them to get away from their everyday lives and enjoy themselves in a nice place. Poor attendance was caused by issues that board members were far removed from: Transportation, attire, and childcare. This further highlights the importance of getting to know the people the organization attempts to serve.

Chapter 5

BATTLE OR BOND?

**If everyone is moving forward together,
then success takes care of itself.**

–Abraham Lincoln

Они were in battle. The leader had to hold the vision for the success of the mission. The story goes, as long as he held his hands up they were winning. But as time went on, the leader's hands grew tired. Two members of his team came to his assistance. They brought him a seat and then these two confidants positioned themselves one on the right and the other on the left. They held the leader's hands steady until the battle was won.[1]

One of the board's most important responsibilities is to hire a chief executive that will carry the organization forward. They'll want the kind of leader who will hold a focus on the big three and stand for it during good times as well as when the organization is facing tough times. This chapter describes our fifth culture shock, revealed when the board and CEO own that they have a joint and equal responsibility, to build, bear, and maintain a healthy working relationship.

---

1   Exodus 17:

The board and CEO connection is discussed as an opportunity to strengthen the organization's capacity by building and maintaining a healthy, collaborative relationship between the two. This is the one chapter in which I make a distinction between the board and CEO. I do so in an effort to indicate how each has a responsibility to strive toward working together as one—one team, same goal, both bearing and owning the responsibility to do so.

Like any meaningful relationship, there may be trials to overcome and opportunities to grow beyond them. It may be a culture shock for the board to accept the invitation to approach the quality of the relationship with the CEO as a choice, a choice that begins before they ever hire the CEO. In a relationship that can easily be contentious, the board will need to decide if their relationship with the CEO will be categorized as – a battle or a bond.

The CEO takes on the responsibility of assuring that the policies and procedures are carried out and the day to day functions are done with satisfaction toward the fulfillment of the mission, all while striving toward the vision and living out the organizational values. The board/CEO relationship holds such an important key to the organization's success that the intentional care over it would be a wise strategic position for both the board and CEO. The relationship between the board and the CEO can be one of mutual respect or a vivid nightmare, and anything in between. We have this discussion here for all too often the relationship often looks like a battle for control rather than a bond established for the good of a worthy cause.

On the one hand, the CEO has the role of leader of the organization. On the other, the board has the role of being the "boss" of the CEO. And while this relationship is prime for tension from a struggle over who's in charge, over whom, it doesn't have to be a hostile connection nor create a controversial environment that sometimes hangs the issues of power and control in the balance of the boardroom.

There is a rising trend toward boards of directors making the decision to remove the CEO as a rapid response to conflict, failed expectations and long-standing feuds between the two. A battle for control seems to have a permanent seat at many a boardroom table often revealed by the board's culture of being quick to flirt with the ultimate power they have to hire and fire. Whether the issue is a poor fit of the CEO's leadership style with the board, strong personality differences, or irreconcilable points of view, the board and CEO both bear equal and joint responsibility for the outcome. Yes, there are certainly times when the CEO may need to vacate the position as a course of action that is in the best interest of the organization. And yes, there can be reasons for a forced change at the top by resignation, early retirement, or an all-out firing.

No matter the reasons behind the CEO suddenly vacating the position, it can be done with decency. And, it can and will be done with respectfulness if the board is grounded in a culture of fair dealings with the CEO as a matter of integrity.

But what about before it gets to this point? Could a more cohesive commitment to working together be the thing that could derail what often ends up being a costly end to the CEO's tenure? The hidden and known costs of turnover in the top position of an organization can be enormous and particularly so when the job is vacated suddenly. The board's journey of hiring a new CEO when the vacancy occurs without advance succession planning, can be a massive undertaking that can hoist great stress on staff, volunteers and the organization's strategic trajectory.

Perhaps you may think this discussion should go without saying but let us speak first to the obvious just the same. The best board/CEO relationship begins with having the right people at the boardroom table making the hiring decision. Here are five indicators that the board is ready for deliberating on the hiring decision:

- the board is clear on its roles and governance responsibilities,
- the composition of the board aligns with the organization's big three,
- the board members are knowledgeable in the organization's affairs,
- the board is anchored to the organization's purpose,
- there is open and honest dialogue as part of the board's culture.

These represent a sound foundation on the board's part for hiring someone who will be a good fit for the board and a CEO they can support as leader of the organization.

The next point that should go without saying, but because it is so often taken for granted, we must address it here. The obvious step of a written job description that has been well thought-out by the board, with input from key staff, and other industry professionals, is often underestimated in importance. The lack of clear expectations of the CEO is an all too common omission and a perfect set-up for a future breakdown between the board and CEO. For some organizations, the job title may say Chief Executive Officer, but what the board really has in mind is "Fixer in Chief." Too often boards fire and hire with an expectation that the new CEO will come in and immediately fix what they perceive as errors left by the previous CEO and board.

Calling the title one thing and expecting something else is the difficult way to go. In preparing the job description the board, most likely through assigned committee work and input from staff, should delve into the needs of the organization. This is the place to spend good energy and effort. If the board is clear about what the organization needs, and the profile of the person who can meet that need they are starting well. However, there is another preparatory step.

Herein we address an issue that may be a shock to the board's culture and challenge the assessment of its actions. If the previous leader left under a cloud of some kind of difficulty, the board will need to own its part in the predicament. Inviting a new leader to step into the old shoes of their predecessor sets that person in the position of starting a new job with a major test – that of working with a board who has not examined their own faults and deficiencies. This is like making the decision to get a divorce suddenly, and then remarrying with no time for self-assessment, reflection or correction of behaviors.

A good marriage counselor would have charged us with taking some time to review what happened, own our part in the break-up, make needed changes with self and then if remarriage to someone who is a good match is the desire, then, by all means, they might say go for it. An important process in hiring the right person, is for the board to assess and evaluate themselves for their level of functioning. This can be done formally with an objective facilitator or informally using computer generated tools followed up with appropriate self-assessment dialogue.

A bit of "self-work" is always a good thing before posting a job position for a new leader. Now, realizing that "self-work" can be difficult, consider the importance of it. The old adage, "It takes two to tango," can help make the point. Not facing up to, and taking responsibility for problems, can be an indicator that history will repeat itself but with a different CEO on the other side. Once the board has done its self-work, identified the current and futuristic needs and wants in the new leader, solid due diligence procedures follow. Just as with recruiting board members the search should yield a good fit for the organization's vision, mission, and organizational values.

Sound preliminary work before hiring a new CEO is where the consequences of the hiring decision begins to take shape. The chances of successfully hiring the right person for the job, will increase by the quality of advance effort made by the board, including a conscious decision of hiring someone with which to battle, or bond. I'm suggesting here that the board make the decision as to its philosophy toward the CEO relationship before the hiring process. What will it be? Battle or bond?

As for the CEO, surely, they will do their own self-work before considering a new position. Unfortunately, far too often this is not done and, in this case, before long old bad habits from a previous job find their way into the new position. The CEO too will want to qualify his or her philosophy toward the board relationship in advance. What will it be? Battle or bond?

Again, there is high likelihood of attracting a good fit for the board, the organization and the CEO when there are solid clear expectations by both parties, which lead us to the written contract. The contract will communicate the choices made by both parties. It could outline landmines for battle and one-sided schemes, or establishing a bond made up of well-intentioned compromises from integrity. Depending on the size of the organization a full human resources development department may not be at the board's disposal. However, there are companies for hire that can assist with proper hiring regulations and guidelines that must be met.

Once the hiring decision is made and enthusiastically confirmed by the vote of the board, a fair and just contract along with any appropriate agreements will be completed. I do know that this is one place in particular that legal consultation is a good idea – on both sides. I used the phrase "fair and just contract" with the intention to draw attention to integrity, ethics, and transparency. The contract and hiring agreements help to set the tone for the relationship between the board and the CEO.

When either side enters into the relationship believing they were in some way deceived, that the agreement is skewed very heavily to one-side over the other, or that the expectations verbally agreed upon have been altered, these are the kinds of things that can ultimately come back to haunt the relationship and generally at the worst time in a very negative way. Conversely, when both sides enter into contract and agreement phase believing the agreement is "fair and just," a positive tone for the relationship is set in motion. A precedent is established for the board and CEO as able to agree under reasonable circumstances.

Once the new CEO is on the job, there is a slight shift in the roles. This begins a time when things are expected to go well. It is the "honeymoon" period, if you will. The problem with honeymoons it that they don't generally last. I made this statement in a workshop once and a woman who had been married for forty years to the same person took issue. She said she and her husband were still on their honeymoon and both very happy in their marriage. Everyone in the workshop applauded. I asked, "Why did we all applaud?" Someone shouted, "Because it's so unusual."

So, in fairness and in tribute to those who prove the statement incorrect I say, "Honeymoons don't usually last." All I mean by the statement is that a honeymoon marks a period that has a definite beginning when the relationship is officially launched and has a definite ending when the newness has run its course. The relationship can go on happily for decades but the "innocence of new" transforms into something else. The "something else" is where the discussion takes us going forward.

The aftermath of the honeymoon often finds the parties involved caught off guard and ill-prepared for what follows. When things appear to be going along fine as is expected of a honeymoon, missteps can go unattended to, weaknesses may be concealed by strengths, and slights are easy to ignore as a gaffe that can be apologized away. All the while, the "something else" is taking shape. What I know now that I did not know in my early days of facing conflict on a board, is that discord doesn't happen in an instant. By the time a situation reaches conflict stage, know this: it has been in the making for some time. So, when immediately after the honeymoon a conflict rises to the surface, this is an indication that during the honeymoon, seeds of discord were planted and nurtured under the disguise and innocent naivety of the honeymoon period.

For this reason, the board and the CEO will want to tend to the relationship with care from day one. In fact, as I have stated elsewhere in the book the board can build a culture of open honest dialogue and this relationship with the CEO should fall under that culture. I hope I am making the point of the importance of getting the new relationship between the board and the CEO off to a sound start—from the beginning. Yes, enjoy the honeymoon phase of the relationship, but avoid the temptation to gloss over the kind of issues that would ordinarily signal a red-flag, or invite inquiry. Open and honest communication can often avert misunderstandings. To try and make the adjustment later can be difficult and often the time for repair has past.

To build on this all-important relationship demands even more attention—support. While one of the board's responsibilities is to hire and evaluate the CEO, that doesn't mean they should sit back and watch and wait to see if he or she will succeed or fail. The board has the responsibility to lend its support for the office of the chief executive. The board can build on the momentum from the "enthusiastic" hiring of the CEO to encourage, embrace and support the person they hired for the job. I believe one of the first questions the board should ask the CEO after hiring them is, "How may we help you succeed as CEO?" This sets a respectful path upon which this new relationship has the possibility to grow into a mutually appreciated partnership. Under this kind of support, the board and CEO will be well positioned to move the organization forward together.

I once facilitated a retreat where the CEO was obviously very near burnout and the board had no idea of her state of well-being. I asked the board about their annual review process and if they thought it was sufficient and effective. The board felt it had done a good job of pointing out the areas where the CEO had accomplished the agreed upon goals and what goals had not been achieved. I asked if they had given the CEO the support needed for successful achievement of those goals that had not been met. An affirmative response led me to ask the unthinkable, "How do you know?"

The question was met with, "What do you mean how do we know? We evaluate her performance every year and tell her where she's done well and where she's not done so well," a member of the board exclaimed.

When I asked the CEO if she felt the board had supported her in achieving the agreed upon goals, not wanting to disturb the board's sense of accuracy, she replied, "There are times when I wish they were more supportive. I don't think they know what it takes to do this job well."

Shifting attention to the board, I asked, "When did you last ask the CEO what she needs in support of her success?"

The response came, "We assume if she needs something, she'll ask."

As we followed the line of dialogue, the board chair turned to the CEO and asked, "What do you need at this point in your job as CEO?"

A good discussion ensued. The result that evolved was that the CEO would have a sabbatical of two months.

Now, let it be said that the board was correct in saying the CEO could well have asked for time off, or whatever she felt she needed. However, the exchange was powerful when the board sincerely asked the question out of genuine care and desire to help the CEO succeed. This could have happened during the annual review process or at any time in between the review.

When such a question is asked, it implies value and appreciation. And, when the board asks, "What do you need from us, that may contribute to your success?" Or "What would be helpful to you in reaching the goals we've agreed upon?" This comes across as a signal to the CEO that they have the support of the board which, can be a boost of encouragement to the CEO and the relationship between the two. It also implies that the board wants the CEO to succeed. Of course, these kinds of questions must be followed up with the results of the conversation. And, yes, the CEO must be willing to be honest with the board, and the board open enough to hear and respond sincerely. This level of connecting happens over time and with ongoing effort toward building relationships around the boardroom table that grow into mutual respect, trust, and appreciation.

In the opening story of this chapter the story is told of the leader, let's call him the CEO, who was fighting the battle facing his community all alone. Sure, he could have yelled out to his team, "Hey you guys I need help can you get over here right away?" An alternative was what happened in the story. Two team members showed up, let's just say they were board members who showed up on the scene, provided help overcoming a significant urgency in getting through a challenge the leader faced on behalf of the sustainability of the community. They stood with the leader in support of his actions, one on each side so says the story. With their support, they held the leader's hands steady and the battle was won.

What could easily be missed here is that there must have been a relationship in place, prior to the urgent need, that allowed for this level of support to come into play. Notice in the story, the leader did not have to ask, as the support was there. The board members were aware enough of what was going on with the organization that they could respond with care and support. This is where boards, can make an investment in the organization demonstrated as a vote of confidence in the leader. Here is an opportunity to make a difference in how the CEO performs by way of providing board support.

When the board leaves the CEO to fight the battles of the organization without their support, the fight can easily be lost, with the CEO taking the blame. Of course, the board could say "That's why we pay him or her the big bucks!" Or, we may respond with the phrase, "Hey, its lonely at the top." My point is, it doesn't have to be so. To repeatedly place the leader alone on the front line and in the line of fire can pay a huge toll on them over time. The consequences of this predicament will find the CEO in a position of subtle withdrawal from the board further separating the two, facing burnout and in need of extended time away as in a sabbatical, or losing some of his or her edge in the quality of decisions made in their professional or personal life.

Some leaders will admit to a human flaw we all have. It is well known that when a person is under major stress that this is the worst time to make important decisions. Yet, all too often, CEO's are repeatedly placed in situations where the organization is facing all manner of challenges and find themselves carrying the stress of doing combat alone with the board waiting to hear if the skirmish has been won by phone or email. In the heat of a struggle, we can know that some of the decisions made may not be of the highest quality. When the CEO's stress levels are exceedingly high, with mental and physical energy compromised, they will have to pay the consequences for, and answer for those decisions—good, bad or indifferent.

If the board really owns its responsibility to provide sound moral and professional support for the CEO, board support will be an important factor in facing any challenge. A cooperative connection between the board and the CEO can improve the quality of performance of both. By way of these two often polarized positions making a commitment to teamwork and setting an intention to build a healthy working partnership, makes what can be a divide between the board, and CEO an opportunity for high-quality rapport in and out of the boardroom. As in the opening quote for this chapter reveals, if the board and CEO move forward together, then success takes care of itself.

Finally, before closing this discussion, an important point must be made. This conversation is not about board members micro-managing the affairs of the organization. What we are speaking to is an attitude that creates an environment where the boardroom feels more like board and CEO are playing on the same team – together focusing on the good of the big three. The team approach means everyone has a position to play and each respects the other to do their part. The board has a role, and the CEO has a role. The lines of responsibility must be respected. The board and the CEO want the same thing but cover different aspects of the same initiative. Board meetings that take the tone of a competitive sporting event, separate those sitting around the boardroom table rather than bind them together toward their common cause. As we've already said, the larger the line of division between the board and the CEO, the greater the opportunity for conflict.

Oh, the conflicts that can be overcome or avoided, when the board and CEO are of one accord making a clear decision to operate from the position of choosing to bond rather than battle.

The fifth of seven strategies to amplify the competence and capacity of board culture:

A board culture based on open, honest, dialogue between the board and CEO allows for the development of a team-centered partnership that has its full energy to direct toward achieving the organization's goals.

DISCUSSION STARTERS:

- When did the board last do a self-assessment activity? What value can this type of exercise have for the board?

- Does the board provide the CEO with an annual written evaluation based on clearly described expectations? Was there a discussion asking the CEO, "How may we support you in taking your success as CEO in this organization to the next level?"

- Discuss the current relationship between the board and the CEO.

- Discuss what open, honest dialogue around the boardroom table, is already doing or would do, for the members of the board and CEO.

- Describe how "challenges" facing the organization have been handled in the past and by whom.

- Discuss "self-care" opportunities, available for the CEO? Is there a sabbatical option available at some point in his/her tenure? Does the contract provide for adequate time to step away and gain personal renewal as well as professional development?

- Discuss how the board can fulfill its responsibilities of support for the CEO but not "over-step" boundaries.

PRACTICAL APPLICATION:

After following through on hiring the best candidate as the CEO, give with ongoing care, the moral and professional support he or she needs. The board should join together in times of relationship or team building that include the CEO. A retreat option can foster developing trust and build on the establishment of a connected culture. After a solid working relationship has been established with time, intentional effort and support, discuss long-term planning for the CEO office under the idea of succession planning. Caution, this is done as a planning exercise in concert with the CEO, so as not to invent an implication that the CEO is being forced aside. Get expert help on succession planning if needed. However, a succession will at some point prove valuable as part of the organization's long-range strategies.

Chapter 6

ELEVATE ATTITUDES ABOUT MONEY

**Before you attempt to raise money,
the first step should be to raise consciousness.**

–Eric Butterworth

Imagine you are the coach of a little league team in your community. It's the day before the season's first game. The team has had several practices, but they have not gone particularly well. One of the players says, "Coach, we can't win tomorrow, I don't want to play."

As coach, what is your reaction? What would be your next steps, your response? Really, take a minute to decide what you would do in this case. Now, whatever your course of action, if we were in a board workshop together, we would examine all the responses, and use them to draw parallels or similarities in a discussion around how your board talks about its finances, and more specifically money.

The opening quote to this chapter sets the tone for our discussion. It also describes our sixth culture shock. This is revealed when a board discovers that beyond the financial reports exist a hidden element that contributes to the success or disappointment in money matters – the attitudes of those seated around the boardroom table. There is mental preparation work to be done before attempting to raise money, increase streams of income, start a capital campaign, launch a fundraising effort, or request funding from donors, grantors, and social investors, that boards often ignore. In this chapter I ask you to think of that preparation work as that of raising the attitude levels of positivity or optimism.

So, preparation work is key before embarking on an endeavor for which we will want to claim as a success. The idea is to open a dialogue around the effects of individual and group attitudes that affect the money and finance decisions board members are required to make. It may be a culture shock moment when the board discovers that around the boardroom table there may be a wide gap in attitudes about money. While some may be positive, it may be an eye-opener to discover that some of those attitudes are divisive, conflict-ridden, and that some undermine the success of financial goals and strategies. The discovery is not about casting blame on any one person, but to work toward elevating attitudes about money for the board as a unit.

If you are a person who believes that positivity or one's attitude is important in shaping outcomes and the quality of the path toward achieving those outcomes this conversation will be palatable. However, if a little convincing is necessary let us revisit our opening scenario. Any coach worth his or her salt, in response to a player thinking the team can't win, would gather the team and give that impassioned speech, the pep-talk. Why? Because the coach is attempting to raise the overall optimism of the players toward a winning attitude. The coach knows if one player believes they can't win, speaks it aloud before the other players, this could plant a seed of negativity that may contaminate the attitude of the entire team. If the team goes into the game doubting their ability to win, they go half-heartedly, and giving their best will be a struggle almost assuring they won't win. It is that before the game pep-talk, impassioned speech, the shouting of a winning affirmation, "Yes, we can," that holds the key to the winning edge. Again, getting it in the heads, hearts and minds of the players before they go out on the field is the strategy toward a win.

Now, if you're thinking that this mental influence only works for little league. Consider this example, did you ever hear a song playing, and before you knew it you were singing or humming that song? Perhaps for hours maybe even days afterward? It doesn't really matter if it was a song you knew or liked for that matter. However, it still took up residence in your head and became the driver of the action you subsequently took which was humming it, singing it, and maybe even adding a rhythmic move to it. Whether you intended it or not you became an advocate for the song and very likely from autopilot mode. What we hold in mind has a way of coming through and affecting our words, actions, decisions and the outcomes to situations we face. I read an article some time ago where a young boxer claims he knew exactly why he lost the championship fight to his opponent. He said of this rival who had continuously taunted him in public with harsh negative remarks regarding his ability to win, "I lost because I let him get in my head."

So, what does this all have to do with money, and more specifically money for the mission of your nonprofit organization? When we bring the attitudes that we have sitting around the boardroom table into a discussion about money and finance, we may notice that we are divided in how we think and the opinions we hold. When we intermingle attitudes and opinions around money intersecting them with others from a variety of experience and beliefs, we cannot be sure what we'll get. Before taking on a money raising project effort, the idea is to flush out the thoughts, attitudes, opinions, and perspectives regarding money and the project – first. Let's all get on the same page. Let's put our cards on the table as part of the journey to increase money, improve finances and attract funding for the mission. But let's do it by syncing our attitudes and levels of positivity before the physical effort.

Whatever thoughts and attitudes we hold around money or finance issues will be factored into the money discussion and decisions. We derive our individual attitudes about money from all manner of avenues like the economic forecasts, the organization's current and past financial successes or failures, and our individual personal and professional experiences. Our cumulative beliefs will find their way into the decision-making process. So, here's where good coaching comes in. The coach, who could be the board chair, the CEO, treasurer or any member of the board, will want to assure that the attitudes around the table, the team, all reflect a thorough assessment of the issue or project at hand from a positive perspective – beforehand.

I make these statements reflecting on a personal experience I had as a board member many years ago. Sitting at the boardroom table while a discussion of raising funds was happening, I did the unthinkable. I was not fully present and did not engage. I let my thoughts wander in and out as the same strong voices on the board, expressed their opinions from a made-up mind. I didn't feel energetically prepared for a fight and based on their past performance I would be argued down. I didn't want to be thought of as being disagreeable or negative as I was sure to be called.

Besides, my thinking was that there were flaws in the plan, my real reluctance was essentially my gut feeling that said it was a "bad" idea. Thinking to myself I was conflicted. On the one hand, I was having my own private inner debate, *this will never work.* Yet, I didn't voice it. On the other hand, I knew the organization needed the money, and who knows *just maybe we'd get lucky.* The majority vote won, and the fundraising idea was approved.

Those who spoke the loudest and the longest had carried the decision. I let myself off the hook by thinking, *hey, I'm just one person, my voice, my vote would not make a difference.* This is like the team going out on the field with divided beliefs about the ability to win. With some of the players convinced they can win and others not, the team spirit is compromised. So, when the ball is dropped, a play is missed, the game is lost, the one who didn't believe they could win can say to his or herself, *I was right.* Their unbelief is confirmed, *see, I knew we couldn't win.* That very personal and private moment of separating one's self from the loss, is from a person who did not take into consideration the power of group dynamics in a collective attitude of optimism toward a win.

Well, that fundraising project turned out to be a disaster. But one of the things I discovered later is that there were others at the table who voted yes, but had their doubts, and went along with the idea just the same. It is often a culture shock moment when discovering that when there are fragmented, negative and contentious attitudes in the boardroom they do affect the decisions in financial and all other matters, and their subsequent outcomes. With so many doubting our ability to pull off the project, it was no wonder it hadn't succeeded. We had failed to get in the huddle. In this case, we had failed to gather around the boardroom table, to bring the spirit of team alignment to a level of joint positive expectation.

The coach, the board chair, CEO, treasurer or any other board member, including those of us who did not speak up, had all dropped the ball by not assuring that everyone's perspective was heard and taken into consideration. In a team sport, everyone must contribute, and contribute their best, or the whole team loses. In a team sport, the team will work together best if everyone feels included, valued, appreciated and respected. I have since evolved into the thinking that board service is likened to a team sport. If they've earned a seat at the table, the expectation is that everybody contributes from their talent, skill, and experience so that the whole team owns the win, or the whole team owns the lessons from the loss. It may be part of a culture shock moment for the board to own the lessons as a fully committed team, where everybody wins together, or everybody admits the loss together.

In my work with boards I have come to believe that often a great fundraising or capital campaign effort is success bound or doomed before it is ever launched. The indicators are revealed by the attitudes of those around the boardroom table. To put forth great physical energy without doing the mental work of assuring that all perspectives have been heard, and neglecting the opportunity for objections to be reshaped, re-structured or reconsidered, may tie the board to a fate less than hoped for. Like the coach, raising the vibration of expectation of a win, such as an impassioned "yes we can," should not be underestimated.

Perhaps the impassioned pep talk may look and sound more like an inspirational view of what the success of the project will look like when completed. Or the vision for success is crafted in a way that allows every member of the board to grasp it, driving all to lean in, focusing on giving their best. The energy of enthusiasm should not be underestimated, but rather the norm for all new endeavors. The idea is to position the money-raising initiative for an inspiring victory first by the upfront preparation in the attitudes of those seated at the boardroom table – followed by a roll-out for staff and others that has the board's enthusiastic support.

The money conversation has an even greater importance for nonprofit boards over that of for-profit boards but for a very subtle reason. The label "nonprofit" or "not-for-profit" stamps an invisible branding on the organization that plays out in how the affairs of the organization operate, by staff, CEO and board. I've heard boards say, "Well we're a nonprofit, we don't have any money" or "We must send out letters begging for money if we hope to have funds", or "We really hope that donors will not let us down and give us money to keep things going." This is the very kind of negative speak that is counterproductive to the organization and the organization's finances. No, not all nonprofits think of themselves in this way but for those that do, they suffer from low-esteem and operate like a poverty case. Yes, by governmental rules and structure, an organization must designate if it has profit as a chief aim or not. So, while your structure is classified as a nonprofit or not-for-profit, this is not a license to think of the organization as poor, broke or inferior.

If your mission is for a great cause, your vision is worth striving for, and the organizational values craft a purpose worthy of your time, talent and involvement, then board, staff and CEO should own that the organization's significance and value are not defined by money. The organization may be in a position where more money would be welcome and greatly appreciated, but do not identify your organization as a poverty case hoping to get by from fiscal year to the next. The community you strive to serve deserves a higher thought and intention, and so do you.

Since doing business require that the organization must have money to operate, consider it valuable to maintain an attitude that is receptive to having whatever resources the organization needs to function well. That means an ongoing mindset toward attracting and drawing funds from a variety of avenues. This is having a willingness to discuss and consider potential avenues for streams of income from a variety of sources. When an organization only has one way for money to come in, but many channels for its going out, this can become problematic if the inlet gets clogged or dries up – for example when a grant is not renewed, or a major donor withdraws funding. For this very reason, I'm suggesting that the ongoing board development include activities and discussions around increasing the board's optimism around finances, raising the attitude of positivity around the affairs of the organization in general, and establishing an openness to expanding avenues of funding. Consider making it a part of the board's educational culture to include ongoing training on financial and money matters as an essential approach to board service for the benefit of new and seasoned board members.

Two final points before I give a list of positive attitude-raising ideas and bring this chapter to a close. First, in the recruitment process, have the talk, that is "The Money Talk." Get to the heart of how the candidates view fundraising, capital campaigns, personal donations, fiscal responsibilities, general economic and financial viewpoints from which he or she will be called upon to contribute in deciding money matters on the board. This is the time to bring up any financial disclosures to which a new board member may not be privy to. This could be items such as pending or recent lawsuits, plans to downsize, budget cutbacks, and any matters pertaining to the organization's financial status that do not breach confidentiality. Yes, these things may be indicated in the financial picture that is in writing but here is the suggestion to make sure the new candidate understands and has an opportunity to share thoughts on the subject before taking a seat at the table.

If there is a stated giving requirement for board members, include it in "The Money Talk." Have the conversation so as to clearly express the fundraising and giving expectations of board members. If your board does not require board members to donate, and although there are some very good reasons for doing so, still bring up the conversation, just so everybody is clear as to why there is a requirement, or why there is not. Clarity around money is always, always, always a really good thing.

Second, build the board you need from the board you have. As previously stated, ongoing training and development, coaching, mentoring can all be part of the board strengthening and growing its positive perspective. Growing money for the mission is an exercise in developing, building, growing and raising of the very attitudes of those seated at the decision-making, policy setting, strategic planning table.

The board has the ongoing fiscal responsibility to assure that the organization has the resources to meet the mission, vision and organizational values. To do this well, as may be required in a changing world, there must be an expanding mindset toward continued growth on the part of the board itself. The idea is to keep expanding the mental container that is the ever-increasing levels of aspiration to ways and methods that meet the big three with improved approaches. This can be the key to success in the present, and a life-line to sustainability for the future.

Here are a few ideas to start the ball rolling if you are not already working on raising or strengthening attitudes around money and financial matters on the board level. You may use these or come up with your own. The idea is to actively work on getting board members to dialogue on money and finances from a positive perspective as a collective board.

With as little as fifteen minutes at each board meeting spend time in communication and dialogue:

1. Discuss current economic affairs from the positive viewpoint of generating solutions rather than focusing on them as unsolvable problems. Example: Say the stock market took a downward dive over recent

days. Each member would be asked to contribute to a positive outlook regarding this. One person might say something like, *The Dow went down 200 points, it could have been worse.* Number two might say *Yes, I've seen worse, but I've also seen it rebound.* Number three might say *I've been following economic trends for decades and there seems to be a resilience in those investors who have a strategy and stick with it.* And so on. The rule here is to keep the comments brief, and positive. I repeat brief and positive.

2. Do a visioning exercise engaging the whole board in imagining the vision of the organization fulfilled. Take some time to revel in the enjoyment of the fulfillment and discuss what this might look like, feel like, sound like, etc. Let the discussion take on an inspiring energy that will leave members uplifted.

3. Have a board member share a positive story that highlights the work of the organization in a favorable light. Example: A member on the board of a food bank described an experience where she volunteered at the center. When this board members shared her experience of service with a good friend, the friend, touched by the story made a donation to the organization of one thousand dollars. Take one per meeting allowing other board members an opportunity to contribute and share.

4. Together, dream a big dream for the organization. Bring in pictures, articles, new ideas for the purpose of dreaming bigger dreams for the organization. Avoid getting into *"we can't do that,"* or *"that would*

cost too much." Let each person share their hopes and dreams for the organization – this can help expand the creativity in times of generative dialogue.

5. Whatever you do to lift and maintain optimism levels, it's okay to have fun, laugh and enjoy being on a great team – fun has a way of helping a team stay positive and connected.

The sixth of seven strategies to amplify the competence and capacity of board culture:

The board that makes it an ongoing practice to elevate and maintain positive attitudes around money, builds on the collective wisdom from which high-quality financial decisions can be made.

Discussion Starters:

1. What might be the effect of a more positive attitude regarding the finances of the organization?

2. What suggestions are there regarding ways to keep the approach to money matters more optimistic?

3. Discuss ways a stronger belief in the "big three" might affect the board's overall financial outlook?

4. Are all members on the same page about member giving to the organization?

5. When you joined the board what was your belief about the organization's finances? Has that changed since you've been on the board?

6. Share some of the techniques you use in your own personal life to help remain positive when the news reports negative economic forecasts.

7. At the beginning of the chapter, you were asked about your response to the young player who expressed doubt about the team's ability to win. What would be your response and manner of addressing that situation? Do you see any parallels to how the board addresses doubt or optimism toward financial affairs or new projects to be launched?

Practical Application:

As discussed earlier, have mini, positive "Money Talks." When looking at the financials, address what is there honestly, this is your fiscal duty. After the approvals have been completed, make it a practice to conclude the finance discussion on a positive note. Consciously look for good things to say sincerely and positively. Remember you are building a board culture that welcomes and appreciates a positive, generative, perspective on money and finance as a means of having money for the mission of the organization.

Chapter 7

MANAGE RISK OR RISK GROWTH

**The only thing more expensive
than education is ignorance.**

–Benjamin Franklin

The ABC organization (not their real name), described their situation as facing a time of necessary change. They had been struggling to find a new location, defined by them as right size, accessibility, and price. Despite what had become a lengthy and sometimes contentious effort, they were willing to persist as they believed a new location would be a symbol of progress and growth. So, with their work cut out, they took a weekend retreat. There was some relationship building, time for creative dialogue, opportunities to work through a few issues that needed time dedicated to sound planning.

On the drive home from that weekend they felt clear on the message determined from their efforts. However, they were not so clear on one thing in particular. During their deliberations, they had a revelation. Their revelation introduces our seventh culture shock.

In this chapter we look at attentive stewardship and managing risk as factors into growth, forward movement and sustainability. The seventh culture shock is unveiled when a board discovers how it has been careless in providing sound stewardship over organizational assets, thereby raising exposure to a variety of risk factors and potentially limiting or delaying the organization's ability to grow. Often a board is so busy looking ahead, planning, forecasting toward the future that important matters in the present are ignored. It may be a culture shock moment for the board to give a thorough assessment of how well it has addressed areas that expose the organization to risks of varying kinds, while little attention has been paid to caring for what already is.

While the ABC board knew they would follow what was revealed to them, it was only in reflection nearly a year later that they could see and understand the tangible and intangible insinuations that would allow them to enjoy the fruit from the time well spent on their retreat. After returning from their retreat they noticed that their existing location was disorderly, in disrepair and in some respects unsafe. Only when they looked at what wasn't working, addressed it head on, did they receive the next good thing that followed – they found the new location. It was a lesson in stewardship, managing risk and positioning for growth.

Our discussion here will sound very much like risk management because a great deal of it is. But stay tuned for we are speaking to so much more. We consider here the grave effects that ignoring exposure to risks can have on the organization's ability to grow forward. Failure to manage risks, allows us to turn a blind eye and claim ignorance if that risk is exercised. As indicated in the opening quote for this chapter, ignorance can be expensive. However, it can also be very telling regarding the temperature for forward, upward movement in the affairs facing the board and the organization. The attitude with which we diligently pay attention to details, or not, can pierce sound judgment and decisions, placing the board in the predicament of struggling through qualifying the organization's readiness for the next level of growth. Avoidance can weaken the ability to grow, blocking the very changes required for forward movement. So, while sound stewardship and risk management may not be popular subject matter, herein may well reveal indicators of the board's attitudinal readiness, and mental preparedness to embrace progressive expansion. Circumstances unaddressed can present a test of our sincerity around growth and sustainability.

The unpopularity of discussing and addressing risk could stem from thinking some kind of danger is involved as may be suggested by the very word, "risk." It seems at the thought of the word we go negative and this is understandably so. The real danger behind the word, however, is when we avoid or neglect to face and clarify what we're really being called to address. In our discussion in this chapter, risk invites us to consider taking necessary action to assure we take care of what we already have in assets, reputation and goodwill. In this way, we embrace our stewardship responsibilities, settle obstacles that could risk our ability to grow, and position the organization for sustainability.

Now let us turn our attention to address two topics where both or either when overlooked can adversely affect an organization's growth, sustainability and ability to move forward on goals in general. They are topics that can keep the CEO and the board up late at night and that is precisely why we must address them – hopefully before the effects of ignoring them are on the boardroom table. Let's start with careless indecision.

I can still hear a CEO saying to me, "How can this happen, we're insured!" After a hurricane had devastated their building, they learned that the insurance was inadequate. They admitted that the policy had not been looked at or updated for several years. So, they found themselves holding an insurance policy that did not adequately address their need and left them with a huge deductible. Yes, that's right they failed to take care of what they already had.

Now, because it was a "natural disaster" and people generally feel more compassionate when these things happen, within a year and through donations, they were able to find a new location. But it was a shaky year. The concerns were of a wide range from getting services to constituents, to dealing with employees who had been displaced, and accountability for funding when an organization is in crises mode. It was the kind of year where the CEO and a few board members lost a few nights sleep. This is the kind of situation that forces the board into survival mode, rather than talking about meeting goals and planning for growth which would surely be their preference.

Insurances cover all manner of accidents, and many predicaments that may protect the organization, until it doesn't. This discussion can be a double-edged sword. On the one hand, boards should make every effort to make sure insurance coverages are in place. On the other hand, boards should not be too dismissive and too comfortable about having insurance saying, "Oh, we're not worried about that...we're insured." Even with the best of policies, out of pocket expenses in an accident situation can still be costly. The failure to assure that the protection is adequate for the organization, and that it reflects changed circumstances, demonstrates careless indecision.

But careless indecision shows up in other ways also. A board and CEO I once worked with refused to consider what I suggested as a check's and balances measure around a money matter. Their response, "Well, we trust our bookkeeper to handle all that, he's been with us for years." And, I have to say when I met the bookkeeper he looked very trustworthy, as much as you can tell from shaking a person's hand. But I pressed on to say, "Whether you trust him or not, is not the issue." As board members I attempted to convey to them their responsibility to protect the organization on every front. Having a trustworthy person in place is great, and quite frankly should be a given, but it does not pardon the board from its responsibility.

Again, any time we fail to make the decisions that assure we have protected the organization, this is careless indecision. When we take lightly the idea of taking care of what we already have, we put the organization, and the organizational goals at risk. Here we could say there is great risk to the future of the organization by way of the board's careless indecision and lack of sound stewardship.

Now, we move to a second topic that can keep the CEO and a few board members up at night—bad behavior. Let me introduce this topic by way of bringing up a newspaper article I read not long ago. The article reported that a board of directors was being named in a suit for the accused sexual misconduct of their CEO. It caught my attention. I'm always interested to learn about what a board might call one of their "worst nightmares." I'm interested as a means of learning or being reminded of, how boards can be more effective in their role as organizational leaders. In the case I was reading about, the CEO was being accused of sexual misconduct, but the board was being brought into the suit because it was believed that they had knowledge of the conduct the CEO was being accused of and failed to take some appropriate action under their fiduciary role.

We live in a time where I think boards have become misguided and lax in their understanding about their liability and what it is that they are there to oversee and protect. And, while boards are generally protected by the corporate veil, and directors and officer's insurance, that is no reason to be uninformed or careless when it comes to addressing issues that could leave the organization exposed. I bring this up here because when board members or the CEO are accused of or involved in conduct that could bring unwelcomed attention to the organization, it becomes a serious matter placed in the center of the boardroom table.

The question raised by the lawsuit was whether the board, or any board member had any reason to believe or any knowledge of the actions being brought to accusation. Now, in the case I mention here, the courts will decide the innocence or guilt of the CEO and determine if the board knew. Unfortunately, more and more we are seeing these kinds of news media headlines. I bring up this case under the topic of "bad behavior" not because I am speaking to the guilt or innocence of this CEO or the board. But to highlight that there are great consequences to the organization, board, and CEO whether innocent or determined guilty. In entertainment circles, there is a saying that "all publicity is good publicity." When it comes to nonprofit boards, this just isn't so.

A large for-profit business generally has a bit of an advantage because they may have a legal department, legal defense fund and other avenues of resources to help them navigate the rough terrain of bad behavior by CEO's and board members alike. But for many nonprofits, the time, energy, effort, legal fees, negative attention, and perhaps sleepless nights of board members and the CEO can mount up to levels of overwhelm. So, while good publicity is favorable for the organization, bad publicity can do great damage to the organization's good works in the community.

Additionally, it may cause funders to withdraw support, or donors to stop answering calls from fundraisers, and land the organization in legal battles that tarnish the name of the organization and sometimes key leaders. So herein is my point, the board must have a mindset of managing exposure to all kinds of risks that could challenge the organization's health, well-being, goodwill, and sustainability. I'm calling bad behavior by organizational leaders that which, if brought to light can put the reputation, goodwill, corporate assets, and organizational stability at risk and in jeopardy. For the most part, these are risks that can be managed, at least on a basic level, through ongoing oversight, accountability, ethics, and by the board paying attention to the affairs of the organization and exercising sound judgment.

If boards can overcome the fear of addressing risks, they will begin to position the organization for the growth that can come as a result of taking care of solid foundational areas of the organization. People in general, seem to carry a fear that just talking about negative situations can make them happen, so often times on a personal level we're willing to take a gamble. Let's just avoid the idea that "negative things can happen." This kind of denial is part of our human make-up. We don't want to get life insurance because we feel healthy and think we'll live a long, long time. The fact that some people do live long lives, gives us hope that we will be one of them. And, yes some of us delay making a last will and testament because we want to believe the time is far off when it will be needed.

But think about it, we will all get to make that journey to death's door. We should not allow the fact that we don't know when we'll take that trip, to be our reasoning for not having some kind of plan for cleaning up and clearing up the affairs of this lifetime. Now if your idea is that I just went negative by bringing up death, then I dare say that is just the attitude a board cannot take. The board must be willing to do what it takes to assure that the organization's assets, reputation and good name are protected and managed, as best as is possible. This means looking at the "what ifs" we find difficult to consider. The truth is "things happen." Addressing disasters as they come, as well as attempting to head them off beforehand, is simply part of the job.

Good stewardship and sound risk management tells us to take care of what we already have. Like it or not we live in a time when increasingly litigious issues are handled with attorneys and courts deciding on our fate. And, nonprofits should not feel protected under the status of being in business without profit motives. Any business can be hauled into court for any number of accusations and charges. This is always a lengthy discussion when we discuss this in board trainings as board members seem to hold the idea "That would never happen to us." I am always happy when one of the members on the board is an attorney to add to this discussion. The focus here is not to frighten boards, it is to make them aware that there are great consequences to neglecting the protection of the organization. Heeding this message may be the very thing that could allow a few less sleepless nights for those seated around the boardroom table.

Finally, the board has the responsibility of ongoing education for its members and that education should include the legal, financial and asset protection responsibilities assigned to board service. Additionally, let us be reminded that we live in a time where personal life conduct, can and does, intersect with professional life, particularly for those in the public eye and in leadership roles. Board members and CEO alike should be conscious of the importance of character and be guided in issues of integrity and ethical behavior in their personal and professional life.

The public's level of trust in those who are organizational leaders, government officials, business executives, teachers, clergy and CEO's has taken a hit due to the increase in reported scandals, accusations of misconduct, and all manner of behaviors classified as illegal or immoral. A question I have often asked of boards is, "Can you say that your board members, including the CEO, has signed a Code of Ethics that you believe every member takes seriously?" I've had responses that range from "What Code of Ethics?" to "We signed it a few years ago, I think..." to "Well we all signed it but...". What I'm always hoping to hear and sometimes do, is "Yes, we all signed it, and we are all very committed to abiding by it."

We certainly live in a time when bad behavior is not only on display, in the news—locally and around the world. We can see it on display immediately, and sometimes in real time by anyone who has a phone and access to social media. While being insured may help the organization withstand some of the consequences of careless indecision and bad behavior by leaders, there must be an intentional attempt to manage exposures to such risks head-on. In short, if the organization has a backside, the competent board will make sure it's covered.

The seventh of seven strategies to amplify the competence and capacity of board culture:

When the board assures the organization's assets, reputation and goodwill are adequately protected, they position the organization with the health that will support growth and sustainability.

Discussion Starters:

1. Are there areas regarding protection of assets that may be ripe for review and possibly an upgrade? Does the organization carry insurance protections for its directors and officers?

2. In general, as far as the board can determine, what is the reputation of the organization among constituents? The community at large?

3. What kinds of things does the organization do to build goodwill in the community at large?

4. Is there a "whistle-blower" policy in place?

5. Are there policies in place to address "emergency" situations where board, staff, and volunteers are aware of the procedures?

6. Has every board member, including the CEO signed a Code of Ethics declaration? Is there a general belief that all abide by the code?

7. Discuss the character traits for serving on the board that best align with the mission, vision and organizational values.

PRACTICAL APPLICATION:

In the on-boarding process for new board members, be sure to cover:

- Code of Ethics,
- Conflict of Interest,
- any Codes of Conduct the board has developed.

The full board should do an annual review and discussion of the Code of Ethics before signing. In decision-making processes ask the board, "How will this decision add to building goodwill with constituents, staff, volunteers and the community we serve?"

AS THE WORLD TURNS

From years gone by, I remember a television series called "As the world turns." The television soap opera aired on a major television network for 54 years. It highlighted the lives of a cast of characters who faced change daily with all kinds of twists and turns played out in entertaining and dramatic television style. That show came to an end in 2010, but today, the world still turns. While the movement of the earth around the sun is so slow that we are not even conscious of it in our daily activities, it is moving, and we are moving with it. But there is something different in how we are moving at this time in the history of humankind.

Ideology around how we have, and continue to, evolve in matters of socio-economic, cultural, environmental, demographic and technological changes, leave us in a place unparalleled in human history. The rate of speed by which change is thrust upon us may feel like shockwaves in the boardroom challenging our methods and approaches. In days gone by it was the world turning as usual with effects often barely noticeable.

Today, as the world turns, those needing the kind of services that nonprofits provide has increased at alarming rates and those numbers in many cases are still on the rise. The current progression requires a shift toward greater urgency to champion the many nonprofit organizations that have as their purpose to affect the quality of life for those who need assistance and support in our society. Surely, it is to our benefit as a society to accomplish, some worthwhile movement in the lives of the many who hunger for high functioning communities that lean toward improving the human condition for all. While we can be inspired by the great number of organizations who have a great mission, vision and set of open-minded guiding values, the work can be fierce. With the degree of momentum often appearing not to be in our favor, the ability to affect change for some nonprofits, can be likened to moving at walking speed trying to get a good aim on a fast-traveling object.

In some cases, it's not having the resources needed. Other times it may be not having the buy-in or support from those who could favorably shape and improve the quality of programs and initiatives. And yes, it can be having the board, or organizational leadership governing from distraction or conflict. This book has attempted to provide for the board an opportunity to shift its culture, competence and overall capacity away from defeating measures traditionally experienced, and back to striving toward their cause.

As the world turns, those employed in the nonprofit sector make their way to the daily tasks of giving of their talents to organizations that serve a meaningful purpose in the community. Since in general, the average nonprofit pay scale does not attract those seeking "the big bucks," paid by the for-profit sector, often those who give of their skill-sets do so at a great sacrifice. So too will we find individuals that agree to serve on the board volunteer their time, talent and expertise at a personal and professional cost as well. But why? Whether employed or a volunteer they put a trust in the organization's decision-making body to uphold the ideal of promoting rewarding and uplifting values. They hold some level of hope for making a difference in society and desire to see the organization succeed in its work. So, great responsibility rests on the shoulders of those who sit at the boardroom tables of our time.

As the world turns, the need for sound functioning nonprofit organizations is critical. The boards of these organizations have such a meaningful significance in our society that they are being called to shift their approach to governance and restructure their culture. The demand is a plea for change. Change that compels boards to operate with greater competence allowing them to meet increasing needs for services, while in many cases experiencing a decrease in resources. The work, generated from a board with increased competence and capacity as part of their culture, stands poised to unleash the potential to be proactive in making a difference in the communities that are local, realizing they may well have a global effect.

I close *Boardroom Culture Shock* admitting that there are barriers to building the capacity of the board with a host of issues that can easily place today's boards in an ineffectual stance. I have attempted to overview many of the concerns affecting some of those issues' boards face.

Here is a recap of the seven strategies to amplify the competence and capacity of board culture:

1. Board members anchored in the purpose for which the organization exists, position themselves as a compelling team to champion the mission, vision, and organizational values.

2. Board competence takes an upward progressive shift when it draws forth its mind-power from a diverse board representing a wide range of perspectives and backgrounds, enhanced by a culture of trust, mutual respect and appreciation.

3. Boards that adopt a practice of listening to change indicators position themselves for the flexibility to assume new pathways as an opportunity toward greater impact of the organization's mission.

4. The board can invigorate the decision-making process with fresh perspectives by a practice of thinking beyond the numbers and gathering input from a wider range of people.

5. A board culture based on open, honest, dialogue between the board and CEO allows for the development of a team-centered partnership that has its full energy to direct toward achieving the organization's goals.

6. The board that makes it an ongoing practice to elevate and maintain positive attitudes around money, builds on the collective wisdom from which high-quality financial decisions can be made.

7. When the board assures the organization's assets, reputation and goodwill are adequately protected, they position the organization with the health that will support growth and sustainability.

As the world turns, not all boards reflect a soap opera-like drama, like those that sometimes play out on boards unable to evolve beyond long-standing traditions. But all may benefit from addressing and assessing their culture – this book has presented an opportunity for boards to do just that. The strategies presented offer fresh perspectives on methods to make a greater impact going forward. Herein, boards can own the victory within the aftershocks that reshape their boardroom culture, with increased competence and capacity.

Yes, as the world turns, let us acknowledge that it seems to oscillate between success and disappointment. While the uncertain landscape of change can raise anxiety, those who are willing to stay the course can revel in the steady incremental movements toward possibilities for the better.

May those who serve to make the world a better place, work with confidence and optimism in support of all who give of their time, talent and resources to build communities that honor the aspiration of health and well-being for all. With amplified competence and capacity, may all who are seated around the boardroom table be proud to serve from a culture of hope and encouragement knowing, you are contributing to making a positive difference in a changing world.

ABOUT THE AUTHOR

Charline E. Manuel is founder and chief executive of One Accord Strategies, Inc. a Maryland-based, nonprofit company. She works with other nonprofit and not-for-profit organizations strengthening their board leadership capacity. Charline is an inspirational keynote speaker, presenter, and workshop facilitator. She leads seminars and retreats that empower boards with education and training programs on topics of Inclusive Leadership, Building Board Capacity, Effective Governance and Compassionate leadership, and her signature board program for faith-based organizations, *The Power of One Accord.*

From lessons learned from facilitating her first board retreat in the 1980's and greatly improving along the way, coupled with serving on several nonprofit boards for over the past twenty-five years, Charline developed a passion for helping boards raise their effectiveness through building harmonious and healthy functioning relationships at the boardroom table. She has traveled extensively to work with boards of organizations whose fulfilled missions strive toward a more peaceful world.

Charline completed academic studies at Wayne State University and Webster University earning undergraduate and graduate degrees in Sociology, Urban Studies, and Human Resources Development. She is a graduate of Unity Institute and Seminary and formerly served in the capacity of spiritual leader and pastor for over twenty-two years. Her international work has led her to organize trips for clean water in West Africa, building a school in Haiti, peace immersion at the United Nations mandated University for Peace in Costa Rica, and presenter at the Parliament of the World's Religions.

Charline is the author of six books including *The Power of One Accord: 7 Spiritual Keys to Harness Synergy in the Boardroom.* She has two adult children and two grandchildren and makes her home in Columbia, Maryland.

For more information about Charline and her work go to charlinemanuel.com or oneaccordstrategies.org.

Made in the USA
Coppell, TX
24 November 2021

66365202R20066